Colin Tough is a jo
and Internet pioneer.
career in Scottish newspapers, editing
his first title at the age of 19, before
moving to London and the magazine
industry. Having edited a range of
print titles, he helped launch many of
the UK's first websites before returning
to ink-on-paper magazines as editor-in-
chief of the UK's best-selling weekly.

# Guess Who I Met!

## by Colin Tough

# COPYRIGHT

ISBN: 9798387942914

A Princes Templar paperback

Cover design by David Richardson

Cover images: Shutterstock, The Scottish Sun/ David Kirkby

*For Chris and Alexander*

# PROLOGUE

I stood at the bedroom door and opened it tentatively, clinging to the handle, and slowly pulled myself through to the dark hallway where the phone had been ringing. The others were standing around as the brief conversation concluded, and my mother returned the phone to its cradle.

"He's gone," came her confirmation, puncturing the silence.

A couple of heartbeats later, I sighed. "It's not as bad as I thought it would be."

My dad, Alex Tough, had just died, having suffered a massive heart attack during surgery. At 15 years old, standing in my bedroom doorway with my family gathered in the hall, I was about to grow up far faster than I'd imagined, my life almost certainly now diverging from whatever path it had been destined to follow.

As I'd counted down the weeks to Dad's operation, I'd begun to consider the worst. What if he didn't survive? What would it be like to receive the worst possible news? Now I knew, and it felt somehow less shocking than I'd anticipated.

But it was a message from beyond the grave a few days later that was to have the most impact on my adult life.

Seventeen years earlier, in 1958, Dad had undergone an operation to replace a valve in his heart. Although the operation had been successful, by 1975 he needed a second operation. Knowing the risks, he wrote a letter to the family and left it in his bedside locker, to be opened only if he didn't survive the surgery.

So it was that a few days after his death and that awful late-night phone call from the hospital, the family received his personal belongings, including a small notelet with a tiger cub on the front that folded out to form an A4 sheet of paper. On it, he had entrusted his final thoughts and wishes to me, my mother, my two brothers and their wives.

I climbed the wooden ladder from the hallway up to the cold converted loft of my parents' bungalow, letter in hand. Sitting on the edge of the bed, I began to read Dad's final message to the family.

It began: "This you will be reading only if 'my numbers is up' and I shall no longer be with you, something we all have to face some time or another and I thought it best to leave this short note."

In my mind, I could see him sitting up in his hospital bed the night before undergoing heart surgery, pen in hand. But I found it difficult to imagine how he managed to distil all his thoughts and emotions for his family onto two sides of A4 paper, knowing that, should they get to read it, he would never see them again.

He apologised for not having updated his will since his last operation but explained that the complexity of the document he'd been sent by the bank had deterred him and he "did not want to ask anyone's help in case they thought I was a pessimist instead of as I think a realist!"

Towards the end of the letter, he addressed me. "Colin, stick in at school as I'm sure you have it and can make a good career for yourself provided you work hard mentally & physically."

His final message to us all was, "Whatever happens, keep a good sense of humour which God gave us and always be optimistic NOT pessimistic."

Weeks earlier, after years of public service on the local council, Dad had been confirmed as a Justice of the Peace, so he signed off, "All my love to the seven of you, Dad. A.S. Tough JP (P.S. About my first and last time signing as a Justice of the Peace.)"

Looking back over my adult life, I now realise that letter,

containing my father's positive expectations for my future and his message to always look on the bright side of life, has acted as a spur in a way I could never have imagined as a teenager sitting alone in the attic with tears streaming down my face.

I've always felt guilty that in many ways my father's death freed me to take the path I wanted in life, rather than the one expected of me. Although he didn't say it in the letter, had Dad not died on the operating table, I believe his expectation would have been for me to go to university. In the sixties and seventies, a degree was seen as the best possible launchpad for any career. If Dad had lived, I imagine any deviation from that path would at best have resulted in a huge argument and at worst a family falling out.

In many ways, his dying freed me to follow my own route, which leaves me with confused emotions – I wish I'd been able to share more of my life with my dad, while I'm simultaneously happy I was able to choose my own path in life. A choice that led to a career in journalism that saw me meet an amazing collection of famous and infamous people and witness some extraordinary and sometimes historic events.

Ironically, more than 45 years later and just slightly older than Dad was when he died, I found myself considering the pros and cons of leaving a similar letter to the one he composed before I too faced major surgery, but I'll get to that later.

First, let's start at the very beginning…

# CHAPTER 1

I was born just two months before the black-and-white fifties turned into the psychedelic sixties, and I was a complete mistake. I'd long suspected it, given the large gap between my brother Ian's birth and my own, but my mother confirmed it in no uncertain terms the week after my father died.

"If abortion had been as easy in 1959 as it is today, you wouldn't be here," she confessed to me.

It wasn't as heartless a remark as it might appear, however. The point she was making was that had I been terminated 15 years earlier, she would have had to face widowhood totally alone in the house. So it was thanks to the less liberal mores of the post-war era that she had me for support.

I came into the world 14 years after the end of World War Two, and 18 years after an event that left a horrendous lasting scar on both the people and the landscape of my home town of Clydebank – the Blitz. Even 40 years after the tragedy, as editor of the town's local newspaper, the *Press*, I remember it as a topic of conversation that haunted the burgh.

Over two nights in November 1940, 450 German bombers had devastated the city of Coventry, leaving more than 550 citizens dead. That same pathfinder group led 263 bombers on the attack on Clydebank four months later, with even more devastating results. The attack left 35,000 people homeless, 1,200 dead and more than 1,000 injured. Only seven homes out of 12,000 were left untouched, and the town suffered more universal damage than any other British town or city.

On the night of the Blitz, my father, Alex, was an artillery officer, training troops to fire anti-tank guns at a camp in the Campsie Fells, the volcanic hill range to the north of Clydebank. He watched helplessly from the hills as the bombs dropped and Clydebank burned on the horizon, knowing his family and loved ones were stuck in the centre of a living hell.

Amazingly, given the carnage those two nights of bombing wreaked, the family home received little damage, and my grandfather's butcher shop – which, unusually for the forties, bore a catchy advertising slogan "If it's Tough, it's tender" across its frontage – also survived.

My own first memories were of a more personal family trauma, although not one I could fully comprehend at the time. I was only four when my teenage brother Ian was rushed into hospital. He'd been ill for some time with a medical condition the doctors couldn't diagnose, and one night after work he rushed to the toilet and began to spew up blood. Being just a tiny tot, I recall very little of the events of that night, or the subsequent 16 weeks he spent in hospital, but I do remember the sense of dread that overtook the house.

Ian had his spleen, which had become enlarged, removed, and Mum and Dad were called in to a meeting with a consultant to discuss a possibly life-saving, but risky, operation. They were warned that the surgery was relatively new and that, at best, it was likely to give Ian only a few more years of life. But Dad, being an optimist and with the alternative being the imminent death of his son, agreed to the operation.

The procedure was a success and set Ian on a path away from his apprenticeship as an electrician towards a career in show business. It was to see him team up with his future wife to form a partnership that would host its own primetime TV series, perform in front of royalty and become national treasures in Scotland as the comedy duo The Krankies – but much more of that later.

Ian's illness and long recuperation allowed me to spend more of my very early years with him than would otherwise have been the case, often playing the role of annoying little brother. I did have my uses though, as a fun toy to amuse him and his mates. I remember enjoying being gently swung from the clothesline, clinging on with my tiny fingers, only for Ian's support to be removed and my happy laughs turn to tears as I contemplated the drop to the ground that beckoned as my infant grip began to loosen. That said, I was always rescued just in time.

We lived in a lovely corner bungalow in one of the posher parts of Clydebank, at the time an impoverished town on Glasgow's outskirts. It wasn't until after my father died that I learnt the secret of how we had managed to enjoy a more affluent lifestyle than most other families in the area.

It was a chance remark by my forthright Aunt Jessie one day that gave the game away.

I was round at the block of flats she and two of my other aunts all had homes in, when she mentioned that my dad once owned a small grocery shop, something I was completely unaware of.

"He bought it with some of the money from the Pools win," she told me matter-of-factly.

"Pools win, what Pools win?" I asked, and the full story came out.

It seems Dad had hit the jackpot on the Football Pools in the early fifties, the equivalent of winning the National Lottery today.

"He won a five-figure sum – a fortune back in those days," explained Jessie, who I felt was delighted to be able to tell me something that had been kept from me until then. "He invested part of the cash in a grocery shop. Unfortunately, your dad's natural instinct was to help people in trouble by giving them credit. You can't run a successful business that way in an area like this, so the shop hit the buffers."

The Pools win did, however, explain how we owned our own house, regularly had a new car, and how my parents could send me to a private kindergarten and primary school.

I'd never considered it before but the lifestyle we led, which also involved eating out at restaurants on a Saturday night and holidays on the south coast of England, was not the norm in Clydebank in the sixties. With Aunt Jessie's revelation, it all began to make sense. To this day, I'm unsure why it was never discussed when I was a child. Perhaps my parents were embarrassed by their luck or didn't want their children to feel that money grew on trees.

My mother was always a bit of a snob. There was more than a little Hyacinth Bouquet in her, so it may just have been that she preferred people, including her own close family, to believe that the Toughs' money had been worked for, rather than won.


My private kindergarten education at Dean House, a small school in Glasgow's West End, that the Pools money made possible, actually provided an iconic piece of British comedy memorabilia.

I arrived home from school one afternoon in my neat little red blazer, red cap and grey shorts to find Ian, then in his early 20s, on the settee with what appeared to be a very young girl. It was my first introduction to Janette, who was to become the other half of The Krankies, Ian's wife and my sister-in-law. My outfit that afternoon obviously stuck in Ian and Janette's memory because it was to play a major role in their stage career.

Some years later, after Ian and Janette had begun to play social clubs, they were booked to appear at the Barrow and Furness Labour Club. The club wanted them to fill three slots on the bill but they only had two – a stand-up comedy routine and a Scottish music section, performed in kilts. They discussed using Janette's height to dress her as a schoolgirl who would interrupt Ian's singing from the audience, but then they hit upon the idea of Janette playing a schoolboy instead of a girl.

Ian went into the loft in Clydebank, grabbed an old pair of our eldest brother Alistair's shorts, a pair of Grandpa Tough's tackety butcher boots and my Dean House blazer and cap... and Jimmy Krankie was born. The cap lasted longer than any of the other components of Jimmy's outfit, even outliving Grandpa's boots, which were resoled and reheeled many times over the years.

Even when the cap was finally retired, that's not the end of the story. In 2019, more than 50 years after Jimmy first wore it, the Victoria and Albert Museum in London ran an exhibition displaying iconic props from famous comedians. So my first school cap ended its days as part of an exhibition alongside Dame Edna Everage's glasses, Tommy Cooper's fez, Ken Dodd's tickling stick, Will Hay's pince-nez and Charlie Chaplin's walking stick.


From Dean House, I went on to Hillhead Primary, another fee-paying school financed by the Pools win. The number one action series on TV at the time was *The Man From U.N.C.L.E.* and the most exciting thing about Hillhead for me, and most of the other schoolboys who attended at that time, was that David McCallum, who played Illya Kuryakin, the show's heartthrob secret agent who everyone wanted to be in the playground, was a former pupil.

Hillhead Primary School was an austere late-nineteenth century monolith and many of the teachers shared the characteristics of the Victorian building itself.

I remember those primary school days being very happy ones, playing British Bulldog – a violent physical version of tag – in the playground and roaming the streets of the posh

Byers Road district of Glasgow at lunchtimes. I wasn't an angel but rarely got into trouble for anything major, with one memorable exception.

It involved an early introduction to porn magazines in my final year at primary school. In those pre-internet days, it was almost impossible for a 10-year-old boy to obtain adult material without the aid of an older accomplice. This led to any boy who could produce a "dirty mag", as they were called, receiving a barrow-load of kudos. So when, on one of my regular scouting missions in my brothers' bedroom, I discovered a black-and-white mucky magazine under one of their beds, I knew I had hit pay dirt. The content had no effect on my 10-year-old prepubescent body, but I knew the ownership of the magazine would do wonders for my reputation in the playground.

I rushed into the school the next morning with my precious treasure. Having furtively shown it to my closest allies, one of them, Gordon, asked if he could borrow it, obviously hoping the glory it bestowed on its owner would be transferred to him when he revealed it to his friends at home. As one of my best mates, I was happy to lend the lewd loot to him for a short period.

A couple of days later, all seemed normal as I directed my daily nod to the curious stuffed duck-billed platypus that sat in a glass display case outside the classroom, took my seat and completed registration with the rest of the class. Then, however, things took an unexpected turn. My name was called out by the teacher, and I was instructed to go to the headmaster's office immediately. I had no idea why this unprecedented summons was taking place but I was pretty sure it wasn't going to be a happy meeting.

"Come in, Tough," beckoned the headmaster. "I think you know what this is about," he said.

I didn't!

"It's regarding some magazines?" he proffered.

I continued to stare down past my grey shorts and white knees at my shoes. It appeared Gordon's father had caught him with the magazine and he'd confessed all.

"Where did you get it," he asked.

I had to think quickly, as I couldn't point the finger at my brothers. Glasgow was far from swinging in the sixties, I'm not even sure if it was beginning to rock gently, so I'd have been as good as accusing one of them of being some kind of pervert.

"In a field behind my house," came my reply, impressively quickly. I remember congratulating myself. That's it, I thought, I've admitted to the deed now, the belt is inevitable!

The belt was the preferred weapon of choice for teachers in sixties and seventies' Scottish schools, used to mete out corporal punishment to those who broke the rules. It was a thick leather strap, also known as a tawse, that was forcefully brought down on the folded hands of the errant pupil, often multiple times at one punishment session.

Later, in high school, one of my metalwork teachers inscribed "OXO" on his belt, so the word was visible when a child had been belted. Many of my primary school classmates had been disciplined with leather on skin, but this was going to be my first experience of it – and I was terrified!

Then, however, the interrogation took a strange twist. The headmaster began to discuss "urges". He knew I had "urges", all boys had "urges", it's perfectly normal to have "urges".

I nodded rapidly with each mention of the word.

"Let this be the last time I have to see you in my office,' he said, calling an end to the conversation.

I found myself back outside his door, totally confused as to what had just happened but thankful that I'd been saved by the headmaster's understanding of my "urges"... whatever they were.

That would have been the end of the story, were it not for an amazing coincidence that took place more than 30 years later.

My wife and I were supporting our son, Alexander, at his Under-8s Saturday morning football training near our home in Surrey when a new parent appeared with his own son. I instantly thought I knew the face but couldn't believe that with a distance of 400 miles and 30 years since we'd last met, it was who I thought it was.

I approached the boy's father and held out a hand. "Hello, I haven't seen you before. I'm Colin Tough," I ventured.

"Gordon," he answered, shaking my hand.

As he revealed his surname, I received the confirmation I'd suspected – it was my pal from Hillhead Primary. We were both amazed by the coincidence and discussed our time at primary school together – although I omitted any mention of dodgy magazines! – and caught up on what we'd been doing for the past three decades and what had brought us both to live in the same small Surrey town.

Once we broke apart and returned to watch our sons, I explained who Gordon was to my wife, who has heard the story of my primary school shaming on a number of occasions, and I brought our friend Elaine, whose sons and Alexander were mates, up to date on the tale.

I never saw Gordon at Saturday football practice again. I'm pretty sure the incident with the porn magazine wasn't something he would have remembered, as it was the memory of being interrogated by the headmaster that forever stamped it on my own consciousness. So I can only imagine his bafflement when Elaine, assuming it was a memory that meant as much to Gordon as it did to me, whispered to him as he left the football pitch, "Still hiding the porn mags?"

Those happy primary school days also saw my first and last venture into show business – appearing in *The Music Man* at Glasgow's King's Theatre.

My brother Ian had first appeared in the footlights as a member of the Theatre Guild, Glasgow's famous amateur musical society, long before he and Janette formed The Krankies, appearing in *Charlie's Aunt*, *No No Nanette* and as Liver Lips Louis in *Guys and Dolls*. My cousin, Joan, was still a member, and she persuaded me to audition for *The Music Man* child lead role of Winthrop Paroo.

The musical is the story of a con man who comes to a midwestern US town and sells them outfits and instruments, promising to teach the town's youth to play as a band. He ends up falling in love with the town's librarian and curing her brother, Winthrop, of his lisp.

I failed the audition to play the featured role but won a place in the chorus – although that was probably because of my availability rather than any musical talent.

By the time I had made my stage debut, The Krankies were busy trying to establish themselves on the northern working men's club circuit but were finding it hard going.

The pair had got together by chance. Having recuperated from his emergency operation, Ian had begun to train as an apprentice electrical engineer and had managed to get himself an evening job as a spotlight boy at the Pavilion Theatre in Glasgow. When the theatre's electrical manager was sacked for being drunk on duty, Ian used his limited electrical knowledge to blag the job, and it was there that he and Janette first met.

Janette was already a stage veteran by that time. In the early sixties, the Pavilion was planning a pantomime that featured six children but, wary of local licensing laws, they were reluctant to cast real kids in the roles. A teenage Janette, who had stopped growing at 4ft 5in and who had been taking dancing lessons since she was seven, successfully auditioned for one of the parts and began her career in show business.

Still working her main job as a junior clerk in a telephone company in the daytime, she was such a hit that she was asked to return the next year and the next, and with each subsequent pantomime her role got larger and larger. Strangely, my very first memory of being in a theatre was at one of those pantos. I was often reminded by my mother that when the noise and hilarity became too much for my preschool ears and I began bawling, I was encouraged to watch "the funny little girl", only to reply, "I hate that funny little girl." Little did I know she would end up being my sister-in-law.

When Ian began his backstage theatre role, he took an immediate shine to Janette and would throw her caramels from his lighting box. Before long, the two of them were a couple and their comedic bantering backstage was impressing seasoned Scottish professional funny men, such as Johnny Beattie and Jack Milroy.

Egged on by praise, the pair of them decided to try their luck in the emerging social and working men's clubs in the North of England. These clubs, a few years later parodied in the TV series *The Wheeltappers and Shunters Social Club*, provided a tough but invaluable apprenticeship for the pair, but by 1967, the work was beginning to dry up.

So, when the opportunity of a booking to entertain the German military bases in Germany and Turkey for two months arose, they grabbed it with both hands. That assignment in Turkey introduced Ian and Janette to an amazing character who both fascinated and terrified the eight-year-old me when I met her at their home in the North East of England the following year.

Ian and Janette had somehow managed to get themselves a council house in the new town of Peterlee, and Mum, Dad and I had made the trip south to spend a few days with them. When we arrived, we were introduced to another guest who was sleeping overnight at their house. I recall a slight apprehension when we were first introduced, knowing there was something unusual about her but not being able to pinpoint exactly what it was.

Her name was Terri Rogers and she was a ventriloquist who Ian and Janette had met during their tour of the military bases. When she brought out her dummy, Shorty, I was transfixed. I learnt later that Shorty's suit was fashioned in London's exclusive Savile Row and his shoes were made by the best cobblers in Jermyn Street. Terri treated him like a member of her family.

Things began to get really creepy when Terri stood Shorty, who looked like the evil doll from the Anthony Hopkins film *Magic*, in front of the full-length window that overlooked the lane behind the house, "to watch the other children going home from school".

Terri's ventriloquism wasn't her only talent. She was also an amazing magician, trained, I was told, by a famous Canadian magician by the name of Mandrake (not the cartoon-strip character!). As an eight-year-old, I was spellbound by her sleight-of-hand close-up magic. Still, however, for some reason I was uneasy around her.

After she left the house, Ian revealed to us all that Terri had previously been Ivan Southgate and had recently undergone a gender reassignment operation, known at the time as a "sex change", a few years before. Although I had some problem understanding – this was 1968 and such things were not commonly discussed, especially if you were only eight – it did go some way to explaining my feelings of confusion.

While in Turkey, Terri's talent for magic had actually managed to get Ian, Janette and the cast of their travelling show into a dangerous situation.

The Turkish US military bases understandably tended

to be situated some way from major centres of population. After travelling all day in sweltering heat in a van with no air conditioning, the party arrived at a hotel in the middle of nowhere one afternoon to find the reception full of local men in traditional Turkish outfits smoking hookah pipes. Terri decided to amuse them all by throwing her voice and making cards appear and disappear. The group of locals were fascinated by the act.

Later that night, however, after the show, as the cast began to board their van, a large crowd appeared and began pelting them with bricks. Word had got around that there was a foreign witch in town. As the crowd rocked the bus, thankfully the driver hit the accelerator and the bus sped off to safety.

I have happy memories of trips to see Ian and Janette in their early days as The Krankies, especially of the first show I saw them appear in with a star name that I recognised. It was 1970 at Blackpool's South Pier. They were bottom of a bill that featured comedian Mike Newman, singers Susan Maugham and Ivor Emmanuel, and Freddie and the Dreamers, a group who had enjoyed huge chart hits in the sixties.

The lead singer Freddie Garrity hosted a kids' TV series at the time, *Little Big Time*, and I was a huge fan. After the stage show, the family all went backstage and Ian introduced me to Freddie. I have no idea why but all I could think to say was, "You've got a big nose.' It was hardly the incisive opening comment of someone who was to spend his career as a television journalist!

As the sixties gave way to the seventies, my happy school days and fun-filled holidays were about to be interrupted by another experience that was to make a profound mark on my life.

# CHAPTER 2

Visits to the headmaster's office apart, my time at primary school was a happy one, with many lovely memories, but those halcyon days came to a dramatic halt when I moved to high school.

My journey to Hillhead involved a bus journey into Glasgow lasting 25 minutes and, being so far from home, there was little opportunity to spend after-school time with friends. My brothers Ian and Alistair had left home and I was living the life of an only-child with no pals to play with. In my early days at primary school, I'd spent leisure time with two girl friends who lived in the road, Anne and Fiona. But as we grew older, our interests naturally diverged and I found myself with no close friends at home.

I'm not sure how it came about, but I remember being asked whether I wanted to continue travelling to Hillhead and move up to the senior school or to transfer to the local high school in Clydebank. I can only think it was the lack of a friendship group at home that made me choose to leave Hillhead and start my first year of senior education at Clydebank High School. Whatever the reason, I very quickly came to the conclusion that I'd made the worst decision of my short life.

I remember the excitement of leaving the house on the morning of my first day at "big school", in my smart new brown uniform and cap. By the time I'd arrived home at lunchtime, however, that sense of thrill had been replaced by unadulterated terror.

I, like many other first-years, became the victim of a ritual that many new pupils to the school suffered – dunking. This involved older boys stalking the corridors for newcomers and having trapped their prey, grabbing their heads, forcing them into a toilet bowl and flushing the toilet. A variation saw the huge sinks in the science labs filled with water and the first-year's head being held under as they jerked and twisted to be released. While many newbies were targeted, isolated by my lack of a social circle formed in primary school, I was undoubtedly easy game for the roving torture squads.

Sobbing quietly, I held myself together on the 15-minute walk back to Drumry Road at lunchtime, but I broke down when I got home to my mother, and it took much persuasion for me to return in the afternoon. After a few weeks, the novelty wore off and the older boys returned to fighting among themselves.

A new nightmare, however, was about to start.

It's difficult to classify or define the bullying that I suffered, as is pinpointing when exactly it all began during my first year at high school. Nowadays it would be known as social bullying. There was no physical aggression involved; it was all psychological and involved two boys, neither of whom I remember having had any real interaction with before the harassment began. It simply seemed to be that they took a dislike to me, for whatever reason, and decided to make my life hell, something they succeeded in doing exceptionally well.

I spent night after night staring out of the attic skylight contemplating how I could escape from my miserable life. I can't say I ever went as far as contemplating suicide, but I can completely understand how children can be driven to such an awful end. I thank God that social media wasn't around in the early seventies, as at least when I returned home it provided some semblance of a safe haven.

After many months of misery, the events came to a head when my parents began to see a change in my personality and I confessed what had been happening over the preceding months. They contacted the school, and the assistant rector – the equivalent of an assistant headmaster in Scottish schools – became involved. The harassment stopped almost immediately and there were no further repercussions for me.

The incident left me with a life-long abhorrence of any form of bullying. I've always been quick to stamp it out if I've suspected anyone working with me was involved in any form of prejudice.

At around the same time I stepped up from primary to high school, I also moved from the Junior Section of The Boys' Brigade (BB) to The Boys' Brigade proper. This was a Christian youth organisation connected to our local church. Both my brothers had been heavily involved when they were younger, and my father had encouraged me to follow their example. It was a Scottish Protestant family tradition, with past members including the likes of former Manchester United manager Sir Alex Ferguson, Scotland rugby manager Gregor Townend, Radio 2 DJ Ken Bruce and Deputy Scottish First Minister John Swinney.

While I'd enjoyed my time in the Junior Section, and I understood and bought into the senior organisation's traditional values of obedience and discipline, I found the weekly meetings where uniforms were inspected, marching drills practised and boys formed into companies, battalions and officers to be too militaristic, while even at that young age I was finding myself questioning the place of religion in my life. Too often in the sixties and seventies in the West of Scotland, I found religion translated to bigotry, and that wasn't something I wanted to be a part of.

I knew that any decision to leave the BB would be met with, at best, disappointment from my father, and at worst, anger, as he saw the organisation as a stepping stone to a stable and righteous adulthood. So after a few years, I announced I was quitting but would return to the Junior

Section as an officer. It was a compromise that my dad and I could both agree on.

My close friend from school, Ronnie Kennedy, made the same switch from the senior BB to become a leader in the Junior Section. Both being fanatical about football, we offered to take on the job of coaching the group's football team and so it was that we met an eight-year-old who later in life was to become a British pop legend and record breaker.

The teams in the Clydebank and District Boys' Brigade Junior Section League were for lads between the ages of eight and eleven – a huge age range for boys at that stage in their development. The difference those three years make to a child's physique is immense. Unfortunately, the bulk of the team Ronnie and I inherited were at the lower end of the age range.

A few of the youngsters showed real skill, but as a result of the age differential in that first season, the team found itself regularly on the rough end of huge defeats, regularly shipping double figures, with the worst of the reversals being by more than 30 goals.

One of the more promising players was a centre half by the name of Mark McLachlan. Mark had arrived to play his first game for the team in a pair of everyday boots, rather than football boots, as he didn't own a pair. One of the other older Boys' Brigade officers managed to lay their hands on a pair of football boots and donated them to Mark so he could play regularly with the other boys.

Years later, when Ronnie and I both lived in London, we met up one evening and he showed me a newspaper cutting with a photo of an up-and-coming young band. He asked if I recognised the lead singer. I stared and stared at the photograph but the face failed to ring any bells.

"The Junior Section football team?" he prompted. "Centre half?"

I looked again and then I began to see who he meant. "Mark McLachlan?" I asked. It was Mark but he'd changed his name to Marti Pellow since forming a band with some Clydebank High School pals.

The group, Wet Wet Wet, went on to have numerous number one hits. *Love Is All Around*, from the soundtrack of the film *Four Weddings and Funeral*, spent 15 weeks at number one in the UK charts, making it the country's best-selling love ballad of all time. In 1995, as a nod to Mark's continued love of football, the group sponsored Clydebank FC, then in Scottish First Division, one level under the top tier.

One of the key tactics I taught Mark and the young squad in that first year of football involved time wasting, not, as is usually the case, to hold on to a result, but rather to stop the opposition from racking up a cricket score. If they were running down the hill to collect the ball, they couldn't be firing it into our net.

Things did improve as the years went on. Three years in, with the bulk of the side now aged 11 and at the top end of the age range, the team made it to the final of the district cup, with the young Marti Pellow putting in a string of man-of-the-match performances along the way.

In the mid-nineties, when The Krankies were top of the bill in pantomime at Belfast's Grand Opera House, Ian was standing at the bar of the city's Europa Hotel when he was approached by someone he took to be a fan looking for an autograph.

"Excuse me," the man interrupted. "I think I used to play football for your brother."

Marti introduced himself to Ian and Janette and they chatted about Clydebank. They've bumped into each other again over the years, even visiting Marti / Mark when he was starring in pantomime in Birmingham.

School continued to improve after the bullying episodes

and amazingly in my final year at high school I was asked to be head boy. I'm pretty sure that it's a role I wouldn't have had the slightest chance of being offered at any other school in Britain, but Clydebank High School (CHS) was different from every other educational establishment in one very important aspect – its rector, John T Robertson.

JT, as he was known, was the man behind the *Bash Street Kids* and many other British comic characters, such as *Tough of the Track* runner Alf Tupper in the *Victor* and footballer *Gorgeous Gus* in *Wizard*. Whether he invented the characters or simply wrote their stories was never clear. However, in his obituary, his son Alistair stated he was their creator, so that's good enough for me.

I first met JT through my father, as they were both members of Clydebank Rotary Club. However, it was only in my later years at Clydebank High, after my dad died, that I really got to know JT. I was never sure how much my appointment as head boy had to do with the bond we had because of my father and how much was to do with some potential he saw in me that even I wasn't aware of. I certainly wasn't given the role because of academic results, as I was neither an outstanding pupil nor a complete washout. I had no great sports talent either but what I did have was a can-do attitude, which I know JT recognised and appreciated.

That can-do attitude, however, saw me involved in a number of "scrapes" both in and out of school.

The year before I became head boy, a huge extension had been added to the old Victorian Clydebank High School building to accommodate more pupils, as CHS had grown to be the largest school in Dunbartonshire. I'd noticed that one small room just off the crush hall, where classes met for registration in the mornings, was unused. The prefects had their own common room but it was busy and noisy and provided very little opportunity to study, so as head boy I asked JT if we could have the empty room by the crush hall as a study room. The request was granted and we moved some tables and chairs in to allow the more studious of the prefects a place of peace to concentrate on their exam revision.

When the new building had been constructed, JT had requested that a squash court be built as part of the sports facilities. As head boy, I'd managed to organise with the janitor, Jim Tate, that I could collect the keys from his office to allow me to sneak into the squash court on an evening to play. Having the keys to the court also gave me access to the entire school, including the prefects' study room, and I had the idea that the room could be used for other more profitable pursuits.

Home brew had become a popular trend in the mid-seventies, with high-street shops offering complete do-it-yourself beer-making kits. I got together a small group of prefect investors, and we pulled together enough cash to buy a brown ale kit from Boots the chemist.

So it was that one night, under cover of darkness, we smuggled the necessary equipment, including a camping stove and a huge bell jar, into the prefects' room in rucksacks and began the brewing process. Using a tin opener, we gently eased the top off the can of malt extract, poured the gloopy syrup into my mother's largest saucepan and added water before lighting a primus stove and boiling the mixture.

A couple of hours later, our job was done, and we secreted the full bell jar in the unit under the sink. Unfortunately, we had no idea what a pungent smell the home brew mixture would produce, nor that it would continue to linger, not just for a few hours but for weeks, as the fermentation process took hold.

Suspicions were raised that illicit drinking had been taking place in the prefects' room but no one realised that alcohol was not being consumed – it was simply being brewed.

The instructions on the Boots home brew packaging explained that the process would take a minimum of six weeks before the beer could be bottled. Impatient as only a teenager can be, we waited exactly six weeks to the day before sampling our hooch. It was dreadful... strong but dreadful.

Each of the shareholders tried the brew but no one wanted a second glass. Our main problem now was how to get rid of the copious bottles of booze without being caught. The original plan was to organise another late-night commando exercise, but when news of our problem reached the ears of Janny Tate, as he was known to the entire school, he agreed to clear the room of all traces of evidence. The janitor enjoyed a drink but whether the beer was poured down the sink or consumed by him remains a mystery.

Janny Tate and alcohol were involved in a couple of other memorable high school scrapes I had.

The first involved a trip to Hampden to watch Scotland v Wales in a qualifier for the 1978 World Cup. I'd organised a minibus to take a group of pupils to the game and asked the janny to drive us over to the other side of Glasgow. The game kicked off at 8.00, so there was some puzzlement as to why the party needed to leave the school at 5.00. What none of the parents were aware of was that a nearly two-hour visit to the Lincoln pub, just 10 minutes up the road from the school, was planned before we set off on the journey to Hampden. How on earth a dozen teenagers travelling in a bus with the name of the school emblazoned across the side managed to get served in a pub, I've no idea, but this was the seventies in Glasgow.

We got to the match just in time for the kick off and, despite the pouring rain that lashed down on us, happily marched back to the minibus having witnessed a 1-0 Scotland victory, thanks to an own goal from Welsh defender Ian Evans.

When we arrived at the bus, parked on a red ash municipal football pitch that was used as a car park on match days, there was no sign of the janny, who had gone off in a totally different direction before the match had started. We waited and waited in the pouring rain, as the pitch emptied of cars and filled with a sea of red water, but still no sign of our driver. With no mobile phones available in those days, all we could do was wait in the teeming rain until finally, offering no explanation for his absence, he arrived to take us home.

Back at the school, thankfully the relief of parents at being reunited with their children, albeit nearing midnight, outweighed the need for a long explanation, as the janny cited engine trouble and his passengers played dumb.


My final encounter with Janny Tate and alcohol involved the annual Remembrance Day celebration in November. The school helped organise the distribution of poppies and collection cans to local pubs and clubs in Clydebank, and after Remembrance Day on 11 November, it was the school's task to collect in the cans and unsold poppies.

I agreed to accompany Janny Tate in the school minibus as we visited bars, hotels and golf clubs to pick up the donations. As the janny was a charismatic character, and we were both on a charitable journey, at each of the watering holes we visited, we were greeted with the offer of a drink. The janny accepted the odd half pint here and there as we went from establishment to establishment, and I was encouraged to join him, despite the fact I was only 17.

Drink-driving laws were lax in the seventies, but even Janny Tate didn't go past two or three pints at lunchtime, and we headed back to the school building with the money. As we drove through the gates, slightly drowsy and with not a care in the world, and I reflected on what the rest of the day held, I suddenly recalled in horror that my mother had booked my first driving lesson for later that afternoon.

What could I do? Explain to my mother that I'd spent the morning drinking on a pub crawl with the janitor and ask her to phone to cancel the lesson, or attempt to get behind the wheel of a car for the first time well over the limit?

I headed straight for my mentor and confidante, Andreana, a young English teacher I'd first met when I was in second year at high school. She had encouraged me to write for fun, in a way I had never considered before, and I can thank her for the successful 45-year career in journalism that I enjoyed.

She had joined the school as a trainee teacher when I was around 13, so I guess she was no more than seven or eight years older than me. She was someone I could both relate to and trust and she was my first port in a crisis like the one I found myself in.

She took me into the staff room and began to make the first of a long series of cups of coffee. By the time the final bell rang to end the school day, I had decided to go ahead with the lesson – a decision I kept from Andreana. Luckily being my first session, very little driving was involved and most of the 30-minute instruction took place in a cul-de-sac, away from any other traffic. It was, I can assure you, the first and very last time I ever got behind the wheel of a car having had a drink.

Ironically, I failed my first driving test a few months later and went on to fail a second one the following year. It wasn't until I was over 30, married with a baby, and had moved to the suburbs of London, that I finally took my test and passed. Karma?

I'm not proud of my actions that day and, to be honest, it was largely out of character for me. Since my dad had died and I found myself as "the man of the house", I'd been a pretty level-headed teenager.

There was one other occasion when I made a reckless decision that went even further and almost resulted in my early death.

My brother Alistair had moved to Rothesay on the lovely Isle of Bute. In the summer of 1976, one of his pals, Billy Lees, was planning to take part in the annual Rothesay to Tarbert yacht race with a crew of mates, all, like me and Billy, inexperienced yachtsmen. He asked if I'd like to join them on his boat, *Blue Eleven*, and I signed on for the voyage.

On the day of the race, it appeared that his friends had had second thoughts and when the last of them pulled out through illness, it seemed our adventure had ended before it began.

That wasn't going to beat Billy though and he suggested that, if I was up for it, the two of us could crew the yacht. Two inexperienced yachtsmen sailing a boat normally crewed by four or five – what could possibly go wrong? I instantly agreed to his proposal.

To add to his recklessness, the sky was darkening and the weather was turning nasty.

It was Billy's final decision that was to prove near-fatal for us both. There are two ways to tackle the race. The first is to take the slower route round the back of Bute; the alternative is to go round the bottom of the island, where the waters promised to be much rougher. Billy chose the latter.

We set off to waves and cheers from my mother, brother, sister-in-law and friends, with the rain pouring and the winds quickening.

By the time the *Blue Eleven* turned west at the foot of the

Island of Bute, the wind was blowing a force eight and it was impossible to see much further than the end of the boat through the rain and cloud. It was at that point, as the force of the sea flooding into the Firth of Clyde hit us, that disaster struck. The tiler began to break away from the boat, before it completely snapped off and was swept away into the grey curtain that surrounded the boat.

Billy and I stared at each other with a look of total panic. Then suddenly, as if awakened from a dream, he shouted to me to grab the flare from the cabin. The hatch was battened down, however. Now up to our knees in water, with a force-eight gale battering us, as the yacht lurched up and down and waves lapped over the top of us, I attempted to unlock the hatch and make my way down the shallow steps to grab the flare stored below.

Tripping at the top of the stairs as the boat pitched in the stormy waters of the Clyde, I tumbled down, smashing my knee as I fell. But I reached the flare and clambered back up the steps to reach Billy at the back of the boat.

"What do I do now," I shouted, finding it almost impossible to be heard above the sound of the storm.

The shrug of his shoulders told me he had about as much idea of how to light a flare as I did, but somehow we managed to send it skywards and signal our distress. It seemed, however, like a fairly pointless exercise, with visibility now down to zero. Who would be able to spot our tiny cry for help?

We battled on, bailing out water much slower than it was filling the boat, in a vain attempt to keep the vessel above water until rescue came.

Then, when all seemed lost, out of the grey mist that enveloped us we saw something and heard a voice through the darkness. We had been saved by the Royal Navy.

Faslane is one of three operating bases in the UK for the Royal Navy and is best known as the home of the country's nuclear weapons. Consequently, the waters around the Firth of Clyde are regularly used by the British Navy for exercises.

We later learned that a frigate had been undergoing regular training, steaming away from our position, when the lookout by chance decided to turn his binoculars around and look behind him at the point when we lit our flare. The ship turned around and sailed to our position. Pulling us alongside, the Navy released a rope ladder for us to climb aboard, lashing the tiny *Blue Eleven* to the ship's massive stern.

Billy and I were given silver thermal blankets to wrap around our soaking bodies and shown to the captain's quarters, where we were offered whisky or brandy to warm us up. As we settled down with our drinks, the captain himself walked through the door. An imposing figure in his royal blue jumper and epaulettes, he got straight to business.

"What's your boat, and where are you out of?" he asked us.

It would be an understatement to say "if looks could kill" when I replied, "Name, rank and serial number only."

The captain made it very plain that he was far from amused at being taken off course to save the life of two complete idiots, and we headed for Tarbet and a reunion with my family in near silence.


The yacht race wasn't my only brush with death as a teenager. Months earlier, I'd been involved in a mugging that almost ended in tragedy.

Although not yet 18, my best mate from high school, Gordon Blair, and I were frequent visitors to a pub in Old Kilpatrick, the next village to Clydebank. While under-age drinking was common in the area in the seventies, most teenagers drank in the Glen Lusset, a small bar that sat on its own almost directly under the towering shadow of the

Erskine Bridge, which joins the north and south of the river Clyde.

Gordon and I, however, preferred The Ettrick. In the seventies, this was a rather ramshackled public house frequented by older drinkers. The floorboards were rotten, and the bar hadn't been decorated in many years, but a real coal fire roared in the corner and music was often played on the fiddle or concertina by enthusiastic drinkers.

Strangely, the pub was owned by Gordon Hogg, who taught French at our high school. Thinking back, it seems very strange that a teacher should have condoned under-age drinking, but at the time it was never considered. Gordon was a descendant of the Ettrick Shepherd, James Hogg, a self-educated farmer who became a celebrated poet and author in the early nineteenth century, hence the name of the pub.

We always regarded it as a safe haven to imbibe on a Saturday night, both from the point of view of our age and any violence that might arise from teenagers drinking.

We'd usually walk the half an hour from Gordon's house to the Ettrick along a tree-lining route out of Clydebank. This was the gateway that led from the urban sprawl of Greater Glasgow tenements to the hills and beautiful countryside of Dunbartonshire and the amazing wonders of Loch Lomond.

We'd return later in the evening by train. Gordon would get off one stop up from Old Kilpatrick, and I carried on two more stops to Singer, the station that served the massive sewing machine factory that dominated the area and, along with the shipyard, employed the bulk of Bankies, as the town's residents are known.

That night, we polished off a number of bottles of Holsten Pils, our usual beer of choice, and headed uphill along the tiny road to the small village station. We were merry as we crossed the pedestrian bridge to the Glasgow-bound platform.

Just as we put our feet on the other side of the track, a gang of lads appeared out of nowhere and began to attack us. I've never been much of a fighter and I was well aware of the fact we were outnumbered, so after the first assailant hit me and I fell to the ground, my first thought was flight, not fight. I rolled over onto my side and jumped down onto the railway line in an attempt to run over the tracks and climb up onto the opposite platform to escape for help in the village.

My attacker, however, wasn't going to let me get away that easily and followed me onto the tracks, knocking me down once more. We rolled about on the lines, as I tried desperately to escape the fight. Such was the intensity of the battle, we failed to see that a Glasgow-bound commuter train was rounding the corner and heading into the station. At the last minute, by some miracle, the momentum of the fight pitched us from the up line to the down line and the train pulled into the station beside us.

Freeing myself at last, I ran behind the train and dragged my body up onto the platform, throwing myself through the closing doors of the train before it pulled off.

The black of the night outside had transformed the train window into a mirror so that as I pulled myself up onto the seat I could see my reflection in the glass. As I opened my mouth, I saw the jagged stumps of my broken front teeth and the blue-and-claret rugby-style shirt I'd just bought earlier that day bloodied and torn.

My first thought was how would my mum react? She had suffered what would now be described as a breakdown after my father had died, crying constantly for over a year, and it was only after a number of sessions with an analyst that she had returned to her normal self. I was terrified what reaction the sight of my beaten-up face and body would have on her.

I climbed the hill from the station and was within sight

of home when I decided to present myself at the Hodges, a neighbouring couple who lived across the road, and ask for help. They rang my mother and invited her across. She was reluctant to go, given the late hour, but when it was mentioned that I was already there, it was enough to coax her. The Hodges managed to clean me up before she saw me, and they also prepared her for what she was about to see. So the reveal was less dramatic than would have been the case if I'd simply appeared at her door.

Some months later, the police got in touch to say my attacker had been arrested in another unrelated case and had admitted to the mugging along with a string of other offences. Strangely, I had the opportunity to claim criminal injury compensation but failed to apply. The thought of having to relive the attack, to complete the form, was too great an emotional strain.

Both the mugging and the yacht incident made the local newspaper, *The Clydebank Press*. I knew the team there well because the year before I'd been asked to write the school column, *High Jinks*, in the paper. I decided from the start that I wanted the column to be something different from the normal school article, which simply listed sports results and parents' evenings. I introduced an element of political satire, comparing activities in the school to real-world events. The young writers and editor at the *Press* enjoyed the contribution it made to the paper, and that was to lead to my first editorship only three years later – but I'm getting ahead of myself!

The school column was a labour of love. I spent much time crafting it every week. Having had my love of writing ignited by my English teacher, Andreana, it confirmed my decision that journalism was the profession I wanted to spend my career in. When I left school in the summer of 1977, I handed *High Jink* over to Christine Jardine, a pupil in the year below, who also had ambitions to be a journalist. Christine went on to work for BBC Scotland and became editor of the Press Association in Scotland, before being elected to Parliament and serving as Liberal Democrat Treasury spokesman under Sir Ed Davey.

Despite my own ambitions to enter journalism, I realised that the chances of getting a job on a newspaper – at the time, the most likely entry point into the profession – were slim at best. So I successfully applied for a place at Glasgow University to read politics. Around the same time, a recruitment ad in *The Sunday Post* caught my eye. *The Post* was, according to *The Guinness Book of Records* at the time, the most read newspaper in the world, enjoyed by more than 80 per cent of the Scottish population. It was a national institution, known for its quirky colloquialisms and comic strips *The Broons* and *Oor Willie*.

The paper, published by the staunchly non-union Dundee-based DC Thomson, was looking for three trainee writers for the Glasgow office. I, like hundreds of others I later discovered, sent in my application. As I said before, I'd been neither a star pupil nor a dunce at school, so I had no reason to believe I would be successful. When an invitation arrived for a first interview, therefore, I was thrilled.

Arriving at the paper's offices in Port Dundas Road, a five-minute walk from the station, I was shown upstairs and led through to the main office, festooned with typewriters and filled with cigarette smoke. The thrill of being in a newspaper newsroom for the first time was intoxicating, and watching the writers at work I knew that was where I wanted to be.

At the end of the office sat the editor and the news editor and to their right was a set of steps down to the library, where my interview with the managing editor, Sandy, took place. I was asked about my application letter and other more general questions about my interests and ambitions before finally being invited to write a feature. I chose to muse on my first trip to the US, the year before, and my impressions of how the country celebrated its bicentennial.

The piece was good enough to get me a second interview and amazingly I got through to the final round of interviews. That took place a few weeks later in the main newsroom and as part of the process, alongside a number of other applicants, I had to sit a multiple-choice paper, which consisted of 20 or 30 moral, ethical and logical questions.

I answered all the questions as I believed DC Thomson would want them answered, not necessarily giving the answer I personally would choose. One for example asked, "If you discovered you had only a few months to live, what would you do?" The answer "Put my affairs in order" sat amongst other more appealing answers such as "Go on a round-the-world trip". I dutifully ticked the boxes I felt they wanted to hear, worrying constantly that each one was a trick question.

They obviously weren't, however, because I received a letter a few days later telling me I'd been successful and offering me a starting date at the salary of £30 a month. I wrote to the university and turned down their offer to take up the politics course. As I've explained, it's a decision I suspect would have been much more difficult if my dad had still been alive, as I'm sure he would have believed a university degree trumped an early start in journalism. But events had afforded me the ability to make the decision myself. I was going to be a journalist!

The story has a bizarre sequel 25 years later.

As editor of a website devoted to television, I was keen to meet all three major party leaders contesting the 2001 General Election for an article that was to compare their TV viewing likes and dislikes. But as the election neared, it became obvious that I was only going to get one face-to-face interview and that the other leaders would have to be questioned by email.

So it was that I found myself in a modest dark wood-panelled office in the House of Commons opposite the Right Honourable Charles Kennedy MP, leader of the Liberal Democrats and, as I discovered, an alternate version of me.

We began the interview by reminiscing about early TV memories. I'm less than a month older than Charles and we discussed *Doctor Who*, *Mission Impossible* and *Stingray*, the Gerry Anderson puppet series set in a city beneath the ocean. I embarrassingly confessed to having had such a crush on one of the characters, Atlanta, when I was six, that I used to sneak over and kiss the television when my parents were out the room.

Charles relaxed into the conversation, one leg on the small red velvet settee, the other trailing on the floor as he drank from a can of Coke.

We ran through more childhood TV memories. He claimed to remember the JFK assassination, which somehow passed by the four-year-old me, but we both had thrilling recollections of Neil Armstrong landing on the moon. We reminisced about the early seventies before reaching our late teenage years, when we both left school.

"I wanted to be a journalist but failed to get a job," confessed Charles. "I ended up studying politics at Glasgow University instead."

"That's funny," I responded, "I was due to study politics at Glasgow but I answered an ad for a trainee writer in *The Sunday Post* and got the job."

I told him that the selection process had involved a series of interviews and writing exercises and that, probably due to *The Post* being Scotland's best-selling paper at the time, the number of candidates for the job had been large.

Charles looked over at me, open-mouthed. "How

amazing," he said as he recounted how he too had answered the ad for a writer and that it was his failure to secure the job, after several interviews, that had sent him off in the direction of politics.

Fate had played its hand and dealt Charles and me two different lives, with Charles' ending far too early when his alcoholism killed him only 14 years after our conversation, at the young age of 55.

# CHAPTER 3

While I was taking my first tentative steps into the world of work, Ian and Janette's career as The Krankies was beginning to really take off.

Their reputation was growing and they had moved up a division from working men's clubs to star in the many cabaret rooms that were popping up across the country in the seventies. These massive clubs packed in huge audiences every night of the week, with venues like Jollees in Stoke-on-Trent holding only a couple of hundred short of 2,000.

Sandwiched between their full cabaret diaries were pantomime and summer seasons. The latter gave me the chance to not only enjoy their shows at night but also to spend time with them and the season's cast throughout the day.

The summer before I started work at *The Sunday Post*, they had been booked for a three-month run at a club in Guernsey.

As always, the show included a group of four dancers brought together for the season. Often, aspiring actresses would take a job as a dancer to join the entertainment union Equity. In those days, an Equity membership card was essential to work as an actor. However, the Catch-22 was that to get an Equity card you were required to have worked a certain amount of time as an actor. Dancing was one way of resolving the paradox, as it gained the artist the experience required to apply for the card.

That summer, the production company had employed four lovely girls for the show, and each one had an interesting family history. One's father was a senior executive at a major city bank, the second's family ran one of the UK's largest flower seed businesses and the third's father headed up the country's largest family brewery.

From the first day of my holiday in Guernsey, I was smitten by the fourth in the group, Fiona. Her father too had an interesting job, having played a senior role in Britain's involvement in the space race, launching rockets from the Woomera Rocket Range in South Australia.

In an attempt to give the impression I was more mature than I was, I told her I was a journalist – well, I was going to be one in a month's time – and after a few days, I plucked up the courage to ask her out.

On the day set for our rendezvous, we met up in the morning and Fiona confessed that at the last minute she'd been instructed to attend a meeting with other members of the cast but that she hadn't wanted to break our arrangement, so had chosen to meet me instead.

We set off on the 20-minute ferry journey east of Guernsey to Herm. It's a tiny island that takes less than two hours to walk round, and we settled ourselves on a golden sandy beach that, with the sun sparkling on the turquoise sea on that warm summer day, could have been the paradise from a bounty commercial, as we enjoyed a lunch of fruit, cheese, bread and wine.

With the beach all to ourselves, we chatted about our lives and dreams, and I was most impressed when I realised the "Neil Armstrong" she mentioned joining her family for dinner was, in fact, the same one who had walked on the moon some eight years earlier.

It was a wonderful day for a 17-year-old with a crush, and thankfully Fiona didn't get in too much trouble for missing the meeting. Unfortunately, my hopes of romance went no further than that island picnic. Fiona's plans to become an actress were a little more successful.

Six years later, after I moved to London and joined *TV Times*, I was chatting to the picture desk team when an illustration drawn for the magazine's cover caught my eye.

I did a double take.

"What's that?" I asked.

"It's a new crime drama called *Widows*," came the reply, as I eyed one of the four women on the artwork.

"Can I see the cast list?"

The picture researcher passed it over to me and to my astonishment I read "Shirley (Fiona Hendley)". The girl on the island had achieved her dream of becoming an actress.

*Widows* was to be one of the biggest TV hits of the eighties, launching the career of the BAFTA-winning writer Lynda La Plante, who went on to write the *Prime Suspect* and *Trial and Retribution* series and many best-selling books.

Fiona became both a National Theatre and Royal Shakespeare Company player and married former Manfred Mann singer and actor Paul Jones, before giving up her acting career to become a Christian speaker.

With the end of that Guernsey holiday, my life in journalism was about to begin.

Five days after my return from the Channel Islands, on Tuesday 19 July 1977, I arrived at work for my first day as a junior reporter on *The Sunday Post*. According to my diary, two days later, on Thursday 21st, I wrote my first story. My memory fails me as to what I did with those two wasted days, but little did I know these were to be my last fallow days for nearly 45 years.

I desperately wanted to be a sports reporter. In the Scottish Press, except for a couple of months in the summer, this meant almost exclusively covering football, such is the dominance of the game north of the border. That wasn't the role I'd been recruited for, however, so I had to bide my time before attempting to make a move to the sports desk.

Like most Sunday newspapers, the job at *The Sunday Post* was split into two parts. Sunday and Monday were days off, and from Tuesday to Friday the team worked on the features element of the paper. On Saturday, the newsroom took on the shape of a daily newspaper, serving up the events of the day for Sunday morning breakfast tables.

Where *The Post* differed from any other Sunday newspaper, in Scotland or beyond, were the centre-spread stories. Anyone with a Scottish heritage of a certain era will remember these quirky tales that filled the middle two pages of the paper.

They recounted events that were strange but true (almost always!) and every writer was expected to suggest a number of these stories every week, from which the editor would choose 10 or 12 to grace the following Sunday's edition.

One example that springs to mind was a golfer who teed off in Fife, saw his ball soar through the air towards a railway line and through the open window of a passing train heading to Aberdeen, resulting in the longest golf drive ever. You get the idea?

Reporters were encouraged to "bash the phone" throughout the week in search of such bizarre nuggets. Along the back of the office sat a line of glass-fronted phone booths, lined with padded walls and air-tight door seals to mute the sound of chattering writers. This was where all phone calls had to be made or taken. I spent much of my first week locked in one of the airless booths, their walls etched with phone numbers and the odd limerick, armed with copies of the Yellow Pages business phone directory, calling piano tuners to inquire whether they had ever found anything interesting down the back of a piano.

"Hello, sir," I'd start. "This is Colin Tough from *The Sunday Post*. I wonder if I can ask you a few questions," before going on to explain my peculiar quest. It was always vital that I got a name, location and age in order to legitimise the story.

Luckily I escaped the initiation prank inflicted on one

naive young writer the year before I joined. The practical joker was Willie Coffey, a laid-back pipe-smoking, bearded reporter in his 30s, who took me under his wing during my early days at the paper. Due to my surname, Willie had nicknamed me "Alf" after the "hard-as-nails" runner Alf Tupper in the comic strip *Tough of the Track*.

Willie had been none too impressed with the know-it-all cocky attitude of the young recruit in question and had set out to teach him a lesson. Phoning from a phone booth at the back of the office, Willie asked one of the telephone switchboard girls to fetch the new boy to answer a random reader's inquiry.

Once the lad was seated in the sealed booth, Willie began his prank call.

"Hello, who would I be speaking to?" asked Willie, adopting a sing-song Highland accent.

"I'm Stephen," came the reply.

"Hello, Stephen. I wonder if you can help me. I have a wee story that I think might be of interest to your readers. It's about a man who comes back from the dead. Would that be something you think would be of interest, Stephen?"

"Yes, yes," the young writer stuttered excitedly. "It would be."

So Willie began his story. "I'm a doctor on a very small island in the north of Scotland and one of my patients has a very rare condition, where his heart can stop and he needs urgent medicine to restart it."

The trainee reporter could be seen through the glass door nodding furiously as he excitedly wrote down the "facts" of the story.

"He has no phone, so when this happens," continued Willie, "his wife jumps on their horse and gallops across two fields to reach my house. I get in the car and drive as fast as possible to their farmhouse to revive him, and she rides back across the fields. So, you see, when his wife leaves their cottage, her husband is dead and when she returns, he's alive. Now would that be a story you think would interest your readers?"

The young teenager excitedly agreed it was very much a story of interest to *The Post* readers, but before he could say anything further, Willie, still pitch perfect as the island doctor, thanked him for his interest and hung up.

"But wait," the youngster screamed down the phone. "Who are you? Where are you?" as the sound of the dialling tone crackled back at him.

I'm told the poor unfortunate spent the rest of his day calling island doctors and relating the preposterous tale before Willie finally revealed the truth.

My own first centre-spread story involved a steward on the paddle steamer *Waverley*, which used to take passengers on day trips up and down the Clyde. A party of 500 from a synagogue had hired the boat for an excursion and had insisted on a kosher meal. Unfortunately, halfway to their destination, Rothesay on the Isle of Bute, the chef realised that in his rush to ensure everything was perfect for the guests, he'd forgotten to organise food for the crew. The chief engineer, however, came to the rescue. Picking up the radio telephone, he phoned his mother who lived in Rothesay and ordered 40 fish suppers from Biagoni's fish shop to be brought to the dock in half an hour.

It was hardly going to win me a Pulitzer Prize for journalism, but it got me off and running.

Another centre-spread story around that time eventually came back to bite me a number of decades later.

The Krankies had been booked to appear in a Hogmanay show on BBC Scotland. Often these shows are recorded, sometimes many months before New Year, and the participants have to merrily ring in the New Year while outside the studio the rest of the world is preparing for

Halloween. This New Year, however, the BBC had decided that the whole affair should be live.

Ian and Janette were appearing in pantomime in Bristol, but a plane had been arranged to whisk them up to Scotland after their afternoon matinee in the west of England so they could make the late-night TV show.

The show took the form of a ceilidh-style event, with the invited audience sitting at tables in the studio as the celebrities performed among them. In the green room, after the show, Ian mentioned that he and Janette had witnessed some strange lights in the sky that night on their flight from Bristol to Glasgow.

The story of a celebrity couple and unexplained lights in the sky seemed like a natural for *The Post*, so I recounted it to one of my former colleagues. Whether something was added in my relating of the story, or embellishments were added at the writing or editing stage, as I must admit was sometimes the case in those days, I don't know. But "Krankies see a UFO" was the story that ran in the paper the next Sunday.

Fast forward now a couple of decades, and my wife, Chris, and I are watching an edition of the news quiz show *Have I Got News For You*.

"Next we have the odd one out round," announced the host Angus Deayton. "Which is the odd one out from the following: Muhammed Ali, Jimmy Carter, The Krankies…"

Chris and I glanced across at each other with puzzled looks. We had no idea what connected Ian and Janette to any of the others. They had to be the odd ones out, we concluded. It turned out we were wrong. The fourth celebrity, whose name I can't recall, was the odd one out because, as Angus explained, "All the others have seen UFOs!"

Ian and Janette also provided me with another middle

page story that was almost as unbelievable but was completely true. It was before they had found national fame as The Krankies, and they were simply described in the piece as "Ian Tough and his wife Janette."

The piece was headed "Ian and Janette nearly died because of a monster eel". I'll let my original words from 1977 tell the story, as they also give you a flavour of how the middle page stories were written...

*IAN TOUGH, Drumry Road, Clydebank, is a keen fisherman.*

*Recently, Ian and his wife, Janette, were in the Isle of Man.*

*They decided to go out for a day's fishing with a friend, David Squires.*

*A mile and a half out of Peel Harbour, all three cast into the sea.*

*Soon David and Ian were doing well but, try as she might, Janette just couldn't get a bite.*

*Suddenly her line jerked. She started reeling in. Something big!*

*It was so heavy, Ian had to help her.*

*Next moment a six-foot conger eel was sprochling in the bottom of the boat.*

*Janette got such a shock as the eel landed in the boat, she bumped into Ian.*

*Ian clattered into David – and, as they overbalanced, the boat capsized.*

*All three were tossed into the Irish Sea.*

*In moments the boat sank, with only the bow sticking out of the water.*

*The three clung on for dear life. But they were being carried farther out to sea.*

*David decided there was only one thing for it. He'd have to swim to the shore, a full mile and a half away.*

*At times he didn't think he'd make it. Every wave threatened to swamp him.*

*Finally, exhausted, he got to the shore.*

*He struggled his way along the street until he reached the lifeboat house.*

*He just managed to gasp out his story before he collapsed.*

*In minutes the lifeboat was launched. It reached the other two in the nick of time.*

*And the conger eel? It swam away to fight another day.*

What's missing from the story is the fact that Ian and Janette were performing a summer season show at the casino in the Isle of Man, and David Squires, Davie to his friends, was their music director. The rest, however, is 100 per cent accurate.

The other element absent from the tale was diminutive four-foot-five Janette's reaction when the trio finally made their way up the beach after their rescue. Thoughtfully, she turned to Ian and Davie and quipped, "Do you realise that when he gets back to his family, that conger eel will say," and she held out her arms, "'Honestly, she was this size.'"

By the way, if you've no idea what the word "sprochling" means, you're not alone – it must have been added by the subs at the editing stage. Short, sharp paragraphs strewn with Scottish colloquialisms were very much a part of *The Sunday Post*'s house style back in those days. Often those left me peerie heidit. [Look it up!]

If Tuesday to Friday at *The Post* was largely all about chasing weird and wonderful stories, things got serious on a Saturday when hard news became the order of the day.

From early morning until late into the night, we would follow news leads, like any other daily newspaper – attending demonstrations, press conferences, serious incidents, and any other newsworthy events.

In the evening, I'd join one of the older reporters on one of two emergency services runs, visiting fire stations, police stations and hospitals, either in the north or south of Glasgow. It was hugely exciting for a 17-year-old, and made me feel like a real newspaper reporter, but it was, at times, also dangerous.

I was usually teamed with one of two experienced reporters, one was Campbell Gunn, who later became spin doctor to Scottish First Ministers Alex Salmond and Nicola Sturgeon and was at one time a member of the Scottish Celtic rock band Runrig.

The other was Colin Blane, who left *The Post* soon after I did in 1979 and joined the BBC, where he had an impressive career as East Africa correspondent, European correspondent and Scotland correspondent. Reporting on the Ethiopian Civil War in 1991, he and Michael Buerke were blown up in an explosion in which the team's sound man was killed and their cameraman lost an arm.

The most frightening night I spent during my own short career as a teenage news reporter was with Colin in a Glasgow housing complex called Red Road Flats.

We'd been sent to Red Road the Saturday after vandals had started a fire in an empty flat and a young 12-year-old boy had died in the resulting inferno.

The complex in the northeast of Glasgow, built in the sixties, consisted of eight multi-storey council blocks, some more than 30 floors high, among the tallest buildings in the city, and the estate housed 4,700 tenants. The area also had a reputation for violent and anti-social crime.

The residents were highly protective of their community, however. Following newspaper stories about tenants being unable to leave the building during the blaze, because lifts had been put out of action by vandals melting the lift buttons with cigarette lighters, and engineers being showered with bricks and bottles thrown down the shaft as they attempted to repair them, the media were not welcome.

Colin and I had been instructed to visit The Rig, the area's only pub, which was bang in the centre of the housing scheme, to research a "colour piece", an article that focussed on how the community was reacting to the fire horror.

It was a warm early September evening as we walked out of the darkness into the windowless building constructed underneath the flats themselves. Designed with a nautical theme that drew on Glasgow's proud seagoing past, it was like walking into a modern-day version of a Wild West pub. The music didn't stop as we walked in and the doors swung behind us, but it felt like there were eyes everywhere trained on us.

After ordering two pints of Tennent's Lager at the bar, we took our drinks to an empty table and began chatting to a couple beside us when a tattooed bruiser made his way towards us.

"You fae the papers?" he asked in an accusing broad Glasgow voice.

"No, we're plumbers working on site," Colin assured him.

"Betta no be, cos if ah catch one of those bastards, I'll fuckin' kill them," the tattooed man promised.

The two of us sat silently, looking him straight in the eyes, and nodded agreement. I couldn't believe the sound of my thumping heart wasn't audible to his cauliflower ears. He stood motionless in front of us for what seemed like forever before finally shaking his head and walking away.

To this day, I have no idea if we were believed or not. But once we had collected a few more quotes for the colour piece, we declined a second pint and made our way, swiftly, back to the office.

In my first couple of months in newspapers, I'd covered a number of minor news events on those Saturday night runs. But what I desperately wanted was a front-page story.

My opportunity came with a murder in Paisley, a town just west of Glasgow. I'd been sent out to cover the report that some toddlers playing outside a close had seen a man being stabbed as he returned from a local shop with his groceries. When ambulance men arrived, his shopping was strewn across the pavement beside him. A trail of blood and broken eggs stained the stairs between the entry to the close and the top-floor flat where he lived.

I talked to the neighbours, who clearly knew him and gave me his identity. I'm ashamed to say, I was cock-a-hoop that I had the story and gave little thought to the poor man's demise.

I rushed back to the office, shouted over to the news editor that I had a murder story for him and began bashing away at my antiquated old Smith-Corona typewriter.

Two hundred words completed, I presented them for inspection.

"So, you've cleared the victim's name with the police then," the news editor asked. I looked back at him blankly. "I'll assume that's a no," he concluded, shifting his gaze to another story on his desk. "You'd better get on to Paisley police, otherwise this is no more than a News in Brief."

I walked away completely deflated. How could I have been so stupid; of course I needed to check the dead man's name with the police. In my mind, I went from ace reporter back to inept rookie in an instant.

I made my way to the phone booths at the back of the office, determined to secure the name of the victim. I asked the switchboard operator for a line and called the Paisley police. "Hello, it's Colin Tough from The Sunday Post. I've just attended the scene of this afternoon's murder in Paisley and wanted to confirm the name of the deceased."

"I'm sorry," came the reply, "we're not releasing that information."

"But, but… I have a name; I just need confirmation."

"I'm really sorry but I can't give you a yes or a no."

Damn, damn, I cursed to myself. So near to that front page story and yet so far… but then an idea struck me. I'd recently watched the film *All the President's Men*, starring Robert Redford and Dustin Hoffman as Bob Woodward and Carl Bernstein, the Washington Post reporters who uncovered the Watergate scandal and eventually brought down President Richard Nixon.

In the film, I remembered one of the reporters asking for confirmation of a name by inviting their whistleblower to hang up the phone if the lead they had was wrong, thus giving tacit confirmation. If it was good enough for Woodward and Bernstein, it was good enough for me.

"OK," I said to my police source. "I'm going to give you a name and if you don't hang up in five seconds, I'm going to run with it."

No answer.

I offered him the name I'd heard from many of the neighbours I'd interviewed. No answer. I counted to five slowly in my head. No answer.

"Thank you, so much," I gratefully declared, hanging up, throwing the door of the booth open and rushing down the office towards the news editor. I told him I had confirmation of the name, but not how I'd secured it.

A couple of hours later, as a huge bundle of the first editions arrived in the newsroom, literally hot off the press, I proudly grabbed half a dozen and headed home to show my mum my story under the headline "Stabbed to death on the way from the grocer's".

It was only later, as I lay in bed pondering my success that the doubts began to run through my head like a squad of police panda cars.

What if the police officer I spoke to hadn't understood what I was suggesting? What if he'd simply been distracted by a colleague for those five seconds? What if they left the phone to answer a call of nature? What if he was just having a laugh? Worst of all, what if I'd named the wrong murder victim?

Understandably, I got very little sleep that night as the possible ramifications of my Watergate-style methodology began to unravel in my tired mind, so I rushed round to the paper shop early the next morning to discover my fate.

I scanned the front of the morning edition of *The Post*, which would have been printed some eight hours after the first edition that had carried my story. The murder was still there, as was the name of the victim. That proved very little, perhaps the police hadn't seen the earlier editions. By this time, I was sure I had the wrong man.

Next, I looked at the front of *The Post*'s main competitor, *The Sunday Mail*. The story wasn't on the front page. Panic! I turned the page, terrified, and there on page 2 was the story of the murder complete with the same victim's name. The relief was amazing, and a huge lesson was learnt.

# CHAPTER 4

Four months into my job at *The Sunday Post*, I got the big break I had been hoping for since day one. A position became vacant on the sports desk, and I became a football writer.

In addition to a love of watching the game, which had grown throughout my adolescent years, in particular since I was a 10-year-old watching the wonderful Brazil side on TV during the 1970 Mexico World Cup, I also had a family connection to the game.

Dad had been a successful Junior football player in Scotland, winning the Scottish Junior Cup with Cambuslang Rangers just before World War Two. The term "Junior" in Scotland refers to the level of football played, rather than the age of the players, and the nearest equivalent in England would be non-league football.

He'd started his career at a local Clydebank club, Yoker Athletic. After just three months on their books, he was transferred to Ayr United in the First Division, then the top tier of Scottish football, making his debut at outside left against Motherwell in December 1935.

When I was young, Dad was a sales manager for a neon sign company, and I have fond memories of listening to stories of his playing career during long car journeys with him on visits to clients during my summer school holidays. A favourite was the gruesome tale of how he lost his front teeth in the centre circle of Parkhead when playing for Ayr United against Celtic.

It was only years later, after he died, when I tracked down a match report in the *Ayrshire Advertiser* dated the week after his first game for United, that I learned a little about his playing style. It concluded that, "One good feature was that young Tough made a satisfactory debut. He was fast, centred the ball well, and it may be taken for granted that he will go into the side [for the next game]."

It also concluded, "He gave the impression that he has speed, crosses a good ball, has a strong shot, and the courage to go through on his own when the opportunity is given."

After his death, my Uncle Bobby told me that this football career had caused a major family rift between Dad and his butcher father, Robert. It appears that both Edinburgh club Hearts and Ayr United wanted to sign Dad in 1935. Robert felt strongly that Hearts offered Dad the best career path, having come third in the First Division behind Rangers and Celtic the previous season. Dad, however, accepted the Ayr offer, resulting in the two not talking to each other for many long months, despite working together behind the counter in my grandfather's butcher shop.

Dad's lifelong love of the game was, therefore, passed on to me by osmosis, so it was natural that when I decided journalism was where my future lay, I would eventually gravitate to football writing.

As well as *The Sunday Post* and its huge stable of comics, such as *The Dandy*, *Beano* and *The Victor*, DC Thomson owned a number of other newspapers.

The midweek *Weekly News*, which largely covered TV and celebrity stories with sport at the back, was a big seller in Scotland, the north of England and Ireland, at its peak in the seventies selling more than 1.4 million copies. In Dundee, where Thomson's head office was, they published *The Dundee Courier* and *The Evening Telegraph*.

As a sportswriter, I was expected to work across all four newspapers and, at times, provide football interviews for the company's comics.

My first few match day assignments were with experienced football writers who were covering Rangers or Celtic matches for *The Sunday Post*, legends of the game like "the Big Man", former Rangers centre half Doug Baillie, and Jack Harkness, Scotland's goalkeeper in the famous 5-1 "Wembley Wizards" victory over England in 1928. My job was to write the minute-by-minute match reports for the Dundee *Evening Telegraph*'s Saturday evening sports edition, *The Sporting Post*.

Every major city had its own version of the Saturday evening paper in those days, usually printed on coloured paper. They were a British tradition, published the minute the games ended, and often before, with the *Stop Press* column on the back page carrying the final score. They fed the fans' appetite for match details long before local radio, and eventually the internet offered kick-by-kick analysis of even the most minor teams. Glasgow had two papers: *The Evening Citizen*, which was printed on green paper, and *The Evening Times*, which was produced on pink stock.

I have fond memories of visiting our local newsagent to pick up the paper as a youngster in the sixties. As the closing credits and theme music of *Doctor Who* faded out on a Saturday evening and the black-and-white BBC globe appeared on the screen, Dad would leap to his feet.

"OK, get your jacket on," he'd shout cheerfully, and I'd smile.

"Won't be long," he'd assure Mum. He'd grab my wee hand and we'd leave out the back door, hitting the cold winter evening air.

From our bungalow, posh by Clydebank standards, it was less than a hundred yards to our destination, a grim bunker-like building that stood alone up half a dozen steps.

Despite the short distance, by the time we arrived our cheeks were stinging red, our fingers numb, as we entered the tiny smoke-filled shop.

Half a dozen men would nod and smile as they welcomed my father. Dad's glasses steamed up as we hit the warmth and he'd take them off to wipe them.

"It's late again," advised a tall man with a cloth cap and muffler.

"Aye," they would all echo, raising their eyes to the heavens. It was the same script every week.

The regular ritual continued. The day's football results were discussed, some gloated about their team's performance, others were ribbed over a defeat. I looked up at the laughing faces, part of the grown-up world.

"At last," our look-out Big Bob would shout, as the van carrying *The Pink* laboured up Clarence Street.

"Ten past six. Ten minutes late again,' would puff one of the waiting throng, as they shook their heads.

"Couldn't it just be that ten past six is the delivery time?" I used to think to myself each week, but I never dared suggest it. What would a six-year-old know!

Once back in the house, my dad would open the paper and read to me the match reports from the teams we followed and the results of games too minor to have been read out on television.

So, a decade after those childhood memories of trips to the newsagent with Dad, I was well aware of the importance of the match details to readers waiting for their sports edition 80 miles away on Tayside.

I was particularly proud when I was sent to cover my first match report from Ibrox, home of Rangers, the team I'd followed since childhood. My dad had taken me to their home ground Ibrox from a young age, and we'd stood on the terracing on the uncovered end of the ground.

We'd park his car a short distance away in one of the tenement streets that surrounded the Govan ground and out of nowhere a young lad would suddenly appear and make the offer to "watch your car, Mister?". This protection racket was an accepted part of the Saturday match ritual and involved Dad paying the boy a small extortion fee when we returned to the car to find it unscathed.

To be truthful, at that young age, the promise of a halftime bottle of Coca-Cola, a beverage not regularly available at home, was as much of a lure for me as the football itself. But I loved standing on the terraces with Dad, swinging on the underside of the crush barriers as he leaned on the metal crossbar above me.

During the Easter holidays spent with my mother's brother, Uncle Arthur, and his family in Stockport, I'd also be taken to see Manchester United, as Arthur was a huge fan. Unfortunately, my first match was in 1970, so I missed seeing the Sir Matt Busby-led European Cup-winning team by just a couple of seasons. The side I watched, despite still containing George Best, Bobby Charlton and Denis Law, was a poor imitation of that all-conquering side that brought the European Cup to England for the first time.

It was managed by Sir Matt's successor, Wilf McGuinness, who had been a promising young United wing half himself until his career had been tragically ended by a broken leg at just 22. He joined United's backroom staff after his injury and Sir Matt anointed him as his successor when he decided to step down as manager.

Unfortunately, Wilf inherited a team on the slide and his spell as United boss was short lived. Years after my childhood visits to Old Trafford, my wife, son and I purchased a corporate package for a United game against Fulham, that included dinner hosted by a very amusing Wilf, who was by then a club ambassador, prior to the match.

I chatted to him about my early memories of the side he led, and he made light of his unsuccessful time leading the team by concluding that he had enjoyed three seasons as manager – autumn, winter and spring!

My first few Saturday afternoon match reports for *The Sporting Post* went well. The earliest edition of the paper was printed just after 4.00 pm, so the first tranche of words had to go through to the paper's copy taker before halftime. This allowed that first version of the paper to hit the streets in time for the crowd leaving the afternoon's matches to buy it on the way home, although it contained information about less than half of the match.

After that, I'd file additional instalments of the report for later editions, right up to the last portion that would include the final score. Each one would simply be a chronological minute-by-minute description of the afternoon's action, running from the announcement of the teams, through to the final whistle.

Each time I had a section to deliver, I'd call up the Dundee number on the large rotary-dial landline telephone in front of me in the press box, tell the copy taker who I was and which match I was covering. They would type out my report word-by-word on their typewriter as I dictated it.

The typed story then went to a sub-editor, who would use a pen or pencil to edit the typed story and send it down to be set line-by-line in metal by a typesetter, at a rate of around 14 lines a minute. Next, the lines of metal were fitted into a chase, the traditional name for the metal frame in which the page is put together, and that was sent to the machine room to be printed on the massive presses.

The whole process was amazingly efficient. The time from my speaking the words to the copy writer until the paper rolled off the presses was kept to a minimum, allowing the paper to hit the streets not much more than an hour after my telephone call.

A minute-by-minute running commentary was the required match-report style for evening newspapers, allowing the story to simply be added to each time the reporter phoned through more commentary for later editions. Morning newspapers required a different style of report, something I discovered I was ill prepared for when I was sent on my first solo mission.

Three months after I joined the sports desk, and having covered a number of Saturday games for the Dundee evening paper, I was awarded a big game for the first time. I headed to Parkhead, home of the reigning Scottish League champions Celtic for the home side's Wednesday night Scottish Cup clash with Kilmarnock.

I was entrusted to phone in a 300-word match report by 9.30 pm, 15 minutes after the match ended, for the following morning's edition of *The Courier*, at the time Scotland's second largest newspaper covering a huge area of the northeast of Scotland.

I arrived at Parkhead in pouring rain more than an hour before the game and slipped into the dry stairwell leading up to the press box. I proudly climbed the steps to the room high above the stadium, taking my seat on the front row of the steeply raked benches. I had a perfect view of the pitch through the massive glass window that stretched across the press box. Plugging in my phone, I wrote the name of the two teams at the top of my lined spiral notepad and waited as the room slowly filled with football writers from other papers.

Half an hour into the game, Kilmarnock went one up, thanks largely to a mistake by the Celtic keeper. Could I be about to report on a major cup shock, I wondered. Still, there was a long way to go and the home side were the Scottish champions.

Halftime came and went, and with 15 minutes to go Kilmarnock were still holding on to their single goal lead. I'd already started to scribble my report into my lined notebook and was feeling very proud of my wordcraft. There had been a one-day rail strike that evening, such industrial disputes being common in the seventies, and I knew Kilmarnock fans would have struggled to make the journey to Glasgow.

So I began, "If they'd had to hitchhike, walk or even crawl to Parkhead last night Kilmarnock fans would not have complained for an instant as they saw their side defeat the mighty Celtic and set up a clash in the next round against Rangers…"

On I went, building more and more of the report on the premise that Kilmarnock had pulled off a massive cup shock. I completed my 300 words. Then six minutes from the end of the game, disaster struck, or rather Celtic defender Roddie MacDonald struck, equalising for his side and destroying my carefully crafted prose.

Panic hit me like a soaking wet leather football in the face. Should I start again? What if Celtic scored a winner? My heart pounded and my head throbbed as I stared down at the now obsolete text in front of me. The next six minutes disappeared in what seemed like seconds and the final whistle was blown.

All my experienced colleagues reached for their phones and began to file their reports. I tore off my earlier scribblings and sat staring once again at the empty lined page.

After a few minutes, as the first of the football writers began to unplug their phones and wave a cheery goodnight to their peers, I began to pull together my report. I still managed to get a mention of the rail strike in. "A goal six minutes from time kept Celtic's Scottish Cup hopes alive last night. With Kilmarnock fans having decided that the only thing between them and a trip to Ibrox for a fifth-round tie with Rangers was another one-day rail strike, Celtic stuck."

The words were once again beginning to flow from my head to my pen, albeit with the other side of my brain screaming at me to speed up. With just the final couple of sentences to complete, the old caretaker came shuffling down the stairs and I suddenly realised he and I were the only people left in the harsh fluorescent lighting of the room.

"I'm just about to phone in my story," I promised him.

"No yer no," he assured me. "I've got a wife waitin' for me at hame. I'm turning the lights aff." With which he flicked a switch and plunged the press box into darkness.

So it was that I found myself outside Parkhead, in the pouring rain, with the ink from my match report running in rivers down my notepad, already past my 9.30 pm deadline. It's hard to imagine, in these days of laptops and smartphones, how isolated I felt that evening, as the floodlights in the stadium turned off behind me and plunged me into almost total darkness.

I began to run towards the lights at Parkhead Cross, the rain pelting down like stair rods and the ink from my notes staining my shirt sleeves as it trickled down the page.

Panting and running, I finally reached two back-to-back red public phone boxes. I opened the one in front of me and was instantly hit by the pungent smell of urine that perfumed most Glasgow city centre phone boxes. I grabbed the phone off the hook, only to discover that the mouthpiece had been unscrewed, rendering it useless.

I dropped the phone, leaving it dangling on its cable, and rushed around to the second phone box hoping for more luck. I heaved the door open and was once again met by the acrid odour of fresh urine; this time it took my breath away as I heaved a sigh of relief – the phone was intact.

It was now nearly an hour after my deadline. I readied my coins, called the copy taker number and it rang out. A voice answered and I inserted the coins. Almost there, I thought, but fate was to present me with one more dodgy back pass. The phone cable had been partially severed and the line kept cutting out – leaving parts of the conversation reminiscent of comedian Norman Collier's faulty mic routine (Google it if you're too young to remember).

Holding my soaking notes, which were rapidly becoming indecipherable, in one hand and cradling the phone under my neck, I attempted to hold together the two halves of the cable as I rapidly garbled my report to a very patient and understanding copy taker in Dundee.

My job completed, I slumped back against the glass door of the phone box. My first solo match report had not so much been a baptism of fire as a baptism of water.

Three months later, Parkhead was also the scene of a sad, poignant moment for me.

It was a Saturday morning and I was on the earliest of the three *Sunday Post* sports desk shifts. I grabbed a plastic cup of Bovril, a drink I'd become addicted to over the previous 10 months, from the vending machine in the caseroom and mounted the stairs up to the newsroom. The long thin office was quiet before nine o'clock on a Saturday and I usually spent the first half an hour of the working day getting up to date with the football news agenda on the back page of the dailies.

I grabbed a copy of the *Daily Express* and was shocked to see they had a football exclusive so big it dominated not just the back page but the front page too. They claimed Jock Stein was about to be sacked from his role as Celtic manager and replaced by his former captain Billy McNeill. The paper contained no statement from the club or Stein but was written by a normally reliable football writer.

Jock Stein was a football legend. His Celtic side in 1967 had been the first British team to win the prestigious European Cup. Between 1966 and 1974 that same team had won nine Scottish League championships in a row. McNeil had been captain of that side, arguably the most successful Scottish team ever, and had left the club after the nine-in-a-row success to become manager of Aberdeen.

The *Express* article explained that Stein's Celtic had

ended the league season in a very disappointing fifth place, while McNeil's Aberdeen had come second to Rangers and that the Celtic board had decided to kick Stein upstairs to an executive position and install McNeil as his successor.

Still stunned by the news I'd just read, I was asked by the sports editor, Ian Bruce, to head out to Parkhead with a photographer, Lawrie, and see what I could find out about the story for a piece in the afternoon edition of the Dundee *Evening Telegraph*.

Lawrie was a much older and more experienced member of staff who I'd worked with during my short period as a news reporter. He and I got on well and we discussed the details of the *Express* front page as we headed across to the East End of Glasgow, neither of us completely convinced that the story held water nor that there would be anyone at Parkhead at just after nine o'clock in the morning to comment on the piece.

We parked next to the only other car that occupied the large car park directly in front of the huge main entrance of Parkhead, and clambered out. Lawrie stood, elbow on top of the car, as I walked over to the twin doors that bore the name "Celtic FC" etched in the glass above them.

I knocked loudly. No reply. Again I hammered at the door. Nothing. After a third rap at the door, I assumed our earlier prediction that the ground would be empty so early on a Saturday morning was correct.

As I turned to walk back to the car, I heard the creak of a door over my shoulder and Lawrie's head began nodding towards the direction of the door behind me.

I turned and looked, and there he was, the great man himself, Jock Stein. Not, as I'd always encountered him before in shirt, tie and suit, but in what appeared to be a golfing sweater.

Senior journalists who dealt with Stein on a day-to-day basis had nicknamed him The Beast. Stories of him making reporters sit for hours in the ante room outside his office were legendary, as were the tongue-lashings he directed towards them.

As a very junior member of the team, I had only ever dealt with him at after-match press conferences, where luckily I wasn't in his direct firing line, and here I was about to ask the most successful manager in British football if his beloved club had sacked him.

"Mr, Mr, Mr Stein," I stammered, "Colin Tough, *The Sunday Post*, err *The Evening Telegraph*. I wonder can you… have you seen the… are you…?"

He held up his hand to stop the flow of gibberish that was fast emerging from my mouth, thus saving me further embarrassment. Smiling, he gently said, "I'm afraid I can't say anything at the moment. There will be a statement at some point."

It wasn't a happy smile, but more the stoic expression of someone resigned to their fate. His demeanour was far from what I was expecting from a man who had hardened journalists quaking in their boots. Along with his failure to deny the story, it left me in no doubt that the story was true. As he turned and walked back towards the doors, I returned to Lawrie standing by the car.

It later transpired that instead of being offered a position on the board, Stein had eventually been offered a management role in the club's Football Pools set-up. He left the side that he had done so much to build into a world-famous team and continued his career as a manager, firstly for a short period at Leeds United and later with Scotland.

Stein died, aged just 62, after collapsing at the end of a World Cup qualification game against Wales in Cardiff. I watched the game and cried when his death was announced. He may have been The Beast to many Scottish journalists, but I'll never forget his kindness to me as an 18-year-old trainee writer who encountered him at the very worst moment of his career.

As a young football reporter, I rarely dealt with the managers of Rangers and Celtic, who were covered by the sports desk's more experienced writers, such as Doug Baillie, so my remit was to report on the next tier of club bosses.

My regular Friday job was to contact as many of those top-flight managers as I could talk to, between them finishing training in the morning and heading home after lunch.

Normally in the morning I'd visit one of the West of Scotland-based bosses at their club ground for a chat and, if I was lucky, a mug of tea. I was always made very welcome by Bill Munro, then in charge of my local team Clydebank, and by Craig Brown at Clyde. Craig went on to become manager of Scotland, and before the nation's qualification for Euro 2020, he was the last coach to take the international team to a major tournament way back in 1998.

Both Bill and Craig were fascinating to talk to about formations and tactics, and it was a real privilege for an 18-year-old football fan to be able to quiz them about the game.

On one particular Friday lunchtime, the flow of advice went in the other direction, and I may have inadvertently initiated a cross-border transfer.

I'd decided to head to Motherwell for my Friday lunchtime chat to hook up with former Rangers centre half Roger Hynde, whose Motherwell side had ended the season midtable in Scottish Premier League.

Still without a driving licence – I'd failed my test twice by this time – I took the train from Glasgow Central Station 15 miles out of town to Fir Park, home of Motherwell, and sat down in the manager's office with Roger, a heavy-built affable guy then in his late 30s.

We discussed the team's plans for the coming season and we both agreed the addition of an extra forward would strengthen the team. As we began considering potential recruits, an idea struck me.

As their ground was a five-minute walk from home, I'd watched a lot of games involving Clydebank in the mid-seventies when they won back-to-back promotions and reached the top division, the Premier League. In those glory days, three players combined to power the Bankies to victory – winger Davie Cooper, who later became a Rangers and Scotland legend, forward Mike Larnoch and striker Joe McCallan.

Larnoch had moved to Newcastle in a £100,000 transfer – a huge fee in those days – but had failed to enjoy the same success he had experienced at Clydebank.

"He's your man," I assured Roger, and I sang his praises, lauding his work ethic and his never-say-die attitude.

The following week, news came through from Motherwell that Mike Larnoch had signed for Motherwell. I never got the chance to ask Roger whether our discussion had influenced him in any way. However, in 58 appearances for Motherwell, Mike only ever netted seven goals. Roger lost his job later that year, and Motherwell were relegated at the end of the 1978-79 season, so I hope he made the decision off his own bat and not due to the encouragement of a teenager's hero worship.


Returning to the office on a Friday afternoon after a face-to-face chat, my job was to call the other Premier League managers to see if I could get a story for the next morning's *Courier*, such as injury doubts for the weekend's games, or, even better, a story for *The Sunday Post*, perhaps concerning a possible transfer target.

Among the bosses on my Friday afternoon list was Alex Ferguson. I'd regularly called him as boss of St Mirren and covered the press conference at which his sacking was announced. Then later in 1978, his name was added to my call list again when he took over as manager of Aberdeen, when Billy McNeill left to replace Jock Stein at Celtic.

I'd love to be able to tell some insightful stories about Britain's most successful manager, who steered Manchester United to 38 trophies, including 13 league titles, five FA Cup wins and two Champions League titles, but to be truthful, I can't. At the time, Sir Alex, as he was to become, was just another Friday afternoon conversation with a moderately successful young manager.

I can say, however, that I remember the conversations being pleasant and non-confrontational, something that couldn't be said of two other Scottish managers who I used to dread calling at the end of each week. Eddie Turnbull was the manager of Hibernian, and Jim McLean held the same position at Dundee United. The pair were at the foot of my list of names to be contacted.

I was so scared of them both that, very unprofessionally, I would call their secretaries as late as possible on a Friday, hoping they'd have left for the day. Both men gave it to you with both barrels if they were displeased and, for some reason, it appeared that was the case most Friday afternoons.

My only consolation was that I only had to suffer their hairdryer approach once a week. The players they led had it relentlessly, as Paul Sturrock, United's Scotland international striker, confirmed to me when we chatted about McLean's management style in later years.

In the same way that Rangers and Celtic managers were the domain of more-experienced reporters, so it was with established footballers. Young reporters like me were encouraged to befriend up-and-coming players, in an attempt to build relationships that would last, when they became the senior players of the next generation.

So it was that I found myself doing the first national newspaper interview with Gary Gillespie, then the 17-year-old captain of Falkirk, during a break from his full-time job in a local branch of the Bank of Scotland, and chatting to Morton's Mark McGhee at the architect's office where he was a trainee.

Both went on to play for Scotland. Gillespie won three English league titles, the FA Cup and the European Cup at Liverpool, while McGhee won four league titles, five Scottish Cups and the European Cup Winners Cup with Celtic and Aberdeen.

The relationship between footballers and reporters in the seventies was very different from the way it is today, as were footballers' attitudes to drinking. I once spent lunchtime enjoying a few pints with a top-flight Scottish striker, who then went on to score two goals against Celtic that evening.


By the start of 1978, the sports editor felt confident enough in my match report skills to let me cover a Premier League game for *The Sunday Post*.

My big break was Patrick Thistle versus Motherwell in the Scottish Premier Division, then the country's top league. Thistle are a Glasgow side who, for more than 100 years, have competed in the shadow of their two great city rivals, Rangers and Celtic, with very few moments of glory. Billy Connolly once said that for years he thought the club's name was Patrick Thistle Nil.

I arrived outside the red brick frontage of the Firhill stadium on a cold March afternoon an hour before kick-off, armed with my "junior report's kit", as the paper's star football writer Doug Baillie always described my pen and notebook.

I climbed the stairs to the section of the stand set aside as the press box, happy to be inside and escaping the wind and rain I'd battled to get to the ground, and plugged the rotary phone provided by the club into the socket under the wooden bench.

I gave a self-satisfied smile. Here I was, 18 years old and reporting on a top-level football match for a major newspaper. I felt so smug.

I decided to celebrate my success. To show off my maturity, I'd light up a cigar. Over the previous few months, I'd taken to smoking miniature Cafe Creme cigars, which came in a small metal tin. Each cigar was about the size and thickness of a cigarette and my father had begun smoking them when the doctor had warned him cigarettes were to be avoided because of his heart condition.

To be honest, I didn't enjoy smoking in any way, but I imagined the cigars gave me an air of sophistication that would help me be accepted by my peers in the Scottish football writing fraternity.

I'd been turned off cigarettes at a very young age by my brother Ian. When I was around eight, he'd let me join him on a trip in his small white van to see Janette at her parents' house in Kilsyth, a 40-minute drive from Clydebank through beautiful countryside. Drives with Ian were a treat that I relished. During the trip, I'd been quizzing him on smoking, badgering him to let me try a cigarette, and he'd finally acceded to my demands.

"Take a deep, deep breath in and inhale as much smoke as you can," he had instructed me, as I tentatively held his soggy rollup between my lips. He slowed the car down to a walking pace, lent across me and flung open the car door.

As the smoke hit my tiny lungs, I gave a loud cough and threw up the entire contents of my lunch. I never considered smoking from that day until I concluded that Cafe Cremes were just the right accessory for my new sports reporter persona.

The cigar I was preparing to light up at the Thistle match, however, was of a different magnitude. Ian had taken to smoking King Edward Swisher Sweet cigars, a sweet-tasting full-sized cigar that tastes like it's been dipped in honey, and I'd blagged a couple off of him when I'd last seen him.

So, feeling very self-satisfied, I sat there in the gradually filling press box, struck a match, lit the five inches of fat cigar and sat holding it, Churchill-like, as the smoke swirled upwards towards the roof above me.

As luck would have it, at that moment Miller Reid, the chairman of Patrick Thistle, came walking towards me. I knew Miller, as he'd studied at Glasgow University with my eldest brother Alistair, and I would often show off to mates by calling over to him when our under-age drinking expeditions took us to his West End pub, Esquire House.

"Miller!" I called out, pretentiously waving at him, fat cigar in hand.

He strolled purposefully towards me, and I was aware that others in the stand were watching us. Perhaps he was going to give me some inside information about the day's game. Entering the row behind me, he leant over and whispered quietly in my ear, "You look a complete c*nt" and then, smiling, he was on his way.

A cigar has never touched my lips from that day to this one.

# CHAPTER 5

By far the highlight of my short career as a football writer was the build-up and aftermath of Scotland's World Cup campaign in Argentina.

While the more experienced reporters in DC Thomson's Glasgow office covered events for *The Sunday Post* and *The Weekly News*, it was traditional for one of the younger writers in the Glasgow office to report for *The Courier* and *The Evening Telegraph* in Dundee. So it was that I found myself at the heart of the euphoria that enveloped Scotland in the summer of 1978.

Scotland had qualified for the World Cup Finals in Argentina from a group of just three with a far-from-impressive set of results, capped by a dubious penalty against Wales that saw us across the line in our final qualifying game.

It was the second World Cup Finals in a row that Scotland had qualified for and, almost as importantly, the second that old rivals England had failed to reach. From that defeat of Wales in October 1977, the hype began to grow, fuelled in large part by infectiously optimistic Scotland manager Ally MacLeod.

I'd met Ally many times when reporting on events at the Scottish Football Association headquarters at Park Gardens. He always had time for a chat, and his exuberance for his role was always clear for all to see.

Scotland undoubtedly had a strong squad that summer, including world-class players such as Liverpool duo Kenny Dalglish and Graeme Souness, but the heights to which expectations grew as 1978 progressed were extraordinary.

MacLeod himself said, "I honestly think that if Scotland, provided that we play a reasonable form at all, we will qualify, and I think a medal of some sort will come and I pray and hope that it is the gold one."

From that statement onward, the expectation that the team would travel to South America and lift the trophy began to grow exponentially as the weeks went by.

I covered the build-up to Scotland's departure, reporting every day from the team's base at Dunblane Hydro, writing news stories and features for *The Post*, *The Weekly News*, *The Courier*, *The Evening Telegraph* and even DC Thomson's sport comic, *Scoop*, often all on the same day.

Being a non-union firm, Thomson's could expect a greater output from its reporters than the unionised mainstream papers. Glenn Gibbons, the *Daily Mail's* celebrated football writer, once asked me why I wasn't dashing off an illustration for the cover of *The People's Friend*, the company's woman's magazine, too. It was hard work but great fun and wonderful training.

Most of the players were very happy to chat, with only one being particularly unhelpful. Graeme Souness had been dating Swedish Miss World Mary Stavin, and the tabloids were pursuing him for personal stories. This may have had something to do with his attitude towards journalists, but I'll always remember my encounters with him as being particularly disagreeable.

Manchester City midfielder Asa Hartford, on the other hand, was the exact opposite of Souness. A thoroughly likeable guy, Asa too had attended Clydebank High School, and, coincidentally, when I later edited the town's local paper, his sister was to become my front office manager.

Asa had first found national fame when a proposed transfer from his first club West Bromwich Albion to Leeds United was cancelled after he was found to have a hole in his heart during the club medical. Three years later, however, he joined City and enjoyed a hugely successful career with club and country.

His Clydebank High connection resulted in me manufacturing a story around him. I contacted the school rector, my old friend John T Robertson, and suggested that following his success with Scotland it would be fitting to make Asa honorary head boy. I assured him I could act as broker in the deal.

I mentioned this to Asa, who was thrilled by the accolade, so a special school assembly was arranged, and I got my exclusive for *The Weekly News*.

As the June start date for the tournament grew closer, expectations swelled to wild proportions, fed by Ally's continued infectious optimism. Fans, now dubbed Ally's Army, were setting off in their droves by land, sea and air, many expecting to see Scotland crowned champions of the world.

At this point, I must confess that, like most of the media, I too was caught up in this grand delusion and, in fact, was also beginning to feed the frenzy.

I'd been asked to cover Scotland's send-off to the tournament at Hampden Park for *The Courier*. It was an event that was bound to dominate the front pages of every newspaper in Scotland, although not *The Courier*. Amazingly, it still carried classified advertising on its front page until 1992, so my "front page" lead was carried in the middle pages of the paper.

The departure was reminiscent of a celebration normally reserved for the winner of a major tournament, with thousands filling Hampden as the players completed a lap of honour, before circling the track atop an open-air bus and leaving the stadium for the airport and their flight to South America.

Watching the events of that evening, I wrote in *The Courier*, "If they had played, and beaten, Brazil, West Germany and England on the same night, Scotland could not have expected such a reception as they had at their

World Cup send-off at Hampden last night." I found myself adding to the hysteria, caught up in the amazing atmosphere.

It was all very different, however, less than three weeks later when Scotland returned from the tournament with their tails between their legs.

It appeared that little or no research had been done on the two minnows in Scotland's group, Peru and Iran, and the team suffered a disastrous 3-1 defeat to the former and a disappointing 1-1 draw with the latter. A thrilling 3-2 victory against Holland in the final match wasn't enough to salvage the nation's campaign, and we crashed out at the group stage and headed home.

I met the Scotland squad at Glasgow Airport on their return. The rain that poured down, soaking the small group of still-loyal fans who had turned up, seemed to make a fitting comment about the nation's drenched hopes.

There wasn't even a wave from the Scotland manager as he sat hunched and drawn in the warmth of the luxury coach.

"What's the matter, Ally, scared to face us," shouted one supporter.

"Lost your tongue, Ally," echoed another.

The country had turned on the pied piper of Scottish football.

Ally himself summed up the zeitgeist. "With a bit of luck in the World Cup, I might have been knighted," he said. "Now I'll probably be beheaded."

A post-mortem was held for the lifeless corpse of Scotland's World Cup dream, and not surprisingly it turned out to be the trial of Ally MacLeod.

The Scottish Football Association held the meeting at their Park Gardens headquarters the following month, and from 9.00 am in the morning I sat around a huge old oak table in a bare basement storeroom surrounded by barred windows with the great and the good of British sports journalism.

We waited… and waited… and waited for a verdict.

Lunchtime came and went, and with every hour the room filled with more smoke from the waiting pack of journalists, until it nipped at my eyes.

I was just 18 and was sharing the table with many of the journalists I most admired, including the doyen of British football writers, Brian Glanville of *The Sunday Times*, and Trevor (later Sir Trevor) McDonald, then ITN sports editor, who sat next to me. For a young journalist, the company and conversation was intoxicating. From inside stories about the great moments in football history to the exploits of one award-winning Scottish writer with a Brazilian prostitute and a roll of Sellotape, I listened, fascinated.

Finally, as the clock in the smoke-filled basement neared seven o'clock, word came that a decision had been reached and that Ally was to remain manager of Scotland. We were all shocked and went our separate ways to file our stories. As a Scotland fan, however, I was incensed. Like many supporters, I had a list of questions I felt needed to be answered by the Football Association.

Why, despite having five months in which to see Peru, did Ally fail to see them once? Why despite weeks of preparation were our dead ball situations so unimaginative? Why was discipline apparently so lax in the Scotland camp? … And so on and so on…

After I sent over my news piece for *The Courier*, my anger made me craft those thoughts into an article, which I filed, unsolicited, to the paper in Dundee. The sports editor printed it word for word. So, aware that many of the SFA's top brass came within the paper's catchment area and were regular readers, I had the pleasure of knowing that as they rose the next morning my questions were being delivered directly to their breakfast tables. I savoured the moment as it was a privilege not afforded any other teenage fan.

Two months later in September 1978, Ally resigned as Scotland manager, ending an ignominious period of Scottish football. Coincidentally, that same month my own job took an unexpected turn that was to change the course of my career completely.

Since my first day as a journalist, I'd been quite certain that I was a writer and that I had no interest in becoming an editor. I wanted to write my own stories, not correct other people's mistakes, I would tell anyone who would listen.

An English journalist, Dave Belcher, had recently taken over editing the sports pages of the Irish edition of the *Weekly News*, following the resignation of the previous incumbent, who had left to join the sports desk on the *Glasgow Herald*. I was asked to train up as Dave's deputy and, believing it to be a good short-term career move that would offer me experience in another field, I accepted.

Weeks later, however, Dave himself resigned to join the *Herald* and I found myself in charge. I had no idea at the time that I would never return to work as a reporter or that it was the start of a 40-plus year career as an editor.

The Irish edition was edited and printed in Glasgow due to The Troubles in Northern Ireland. The paper's printing plant had been bombed, and it was felt that it was safer to move the entire operation across the Irish Sea.

Unusually for Irish newspapers, the *Weekly News* sold on both sides of the border and delivered news and sport from both north and south. Its sports coverage was far more diverse than its Scottish cousin, including rugby, football, hurling and Gaelic football.

Each sport had a dedicated freelancer who wrote exclusively about one sport. This team, based in Ireland, included the BBC's Jim Neilly, who covered rugby and was, at the time, a science teacher in Belfast but later took over from Harry Carpenter as the BBC's voice of boxing.

By far the most colourful character was Paddy Toner, a Northern Irish journalistic legend, who covered football for me.

Despite having a very short apprenticeship under him before he left to join the *Herald*, Dave had left me an extensive set of notes about each of the sports and the writers. It was advice that was to save me on more than one occasion.

The sports pages went to bed on a Tuesday. On the first week under my watch, it was after nine o'clock by the time I had signed off the final ones, making me very unpopular with the typesetters and caseroom workers, who had been used to finishing the issue around five and must have wondered what lay ahead with this teenager in charge. Within a couple of weeks, however, I was getting in the swing of things and the schedule had returned to normal.

Then disaster struck. It was Tuesday lunchtime and Paddy's back-page stories still hadn't arrived. Panicking, I reached for the handbook Dave had bequeathed me when he left.

Turning quickly to the pages devoted to Paddy, I discovered the names of a dozen pubs, each with a time written beside it. In these pre-mobile phone days, it was a list of the phone numbers of bars I could call if Paddy's copy hadn't arrived.

I began by calling the first on the list. "Hello, can I speak to Paddy Toner," I asked.

"He's not here," came the reply, followed by the suggestion of another bar.

It had been next on my list, so I called it.

"Paddy? No, you've just missed him," said the barman, who proposed another Belfast saloon I might want to try.

Frantically I dialled again, watching as the hands of the office clock appeared to race unnaturally fast.

"Hello, can I speak to Paddy Toner," I asked, the words tumbling out.

"Paddy!" I heard the publican shout, "a call for you."

When Paddy came on the line, he was his usual wise-cracking self. He apologised for any panic I'd suffered and offered to dictate his stories to a copy taker immediately if I transferred the call.

I'm pretty sure Paddy would have called in his copy that afternoon, even if I hadn't chased him from bar to bar, as he was a true professional and an excellent journalist. But he was also a great example of the type of newspaper character that was already a dying breed and a time when much of a journalist's work was carried out in smoke-filled pubs.

Just two months after my career took an unexpected turn in a new direction, Ian and Janette as The Krankies gave a performance that was to be a life-changing experience for them, thanks in part to illness striking a member of the royal family.

They had won the British Club Act of the Year, and Princess Margaret had been due to present Ian and Janette with their award at a show to be held in the huge Jollees nightclub in Stoke-on-Trent. Unfortunately for her, but not for them, she had been taken ill and had to bow out of the event. Lord Bernard Delfont, the legendary theatre producer, was engaged to take her place and make the presentation.

The award show was restaged in Cardiff a few weeks later in February, so that it could be filmed for TV, and Lord Delfont made the trip to Wales to reenact the presentation. After the show, Ian and Janette stayed at the same country house hotel as the impresario. In the morning, they were surprised to find a note had been pushed under their door saying simply, "Ring Lord D in the morning."

When they called, they were flabbergasted to be told that, impressed by their act, he was booking them for the Royal Variety Performance in November. The Royal Variety Performance is a charity event attended by a member of the royal family that has been held, usually in a London theatre, since 1912, featuring many of the greatest names in show business, from the Beatles to silent screen legends Laurel and Hardy.

Ian and Janette were told the information was top secret and that if the news was to get out it might jeopardise their appearance. I visited them in Jersey, where they were doing summer season, but not a word was said about their upcoming big break until finally in September the line-up was announced, and the celebrations began. I remember pink champagne flowing at one party that started after their evening cabaret ended and finished with the birds singing and the sun blazing the following morning.

The week of the Royal Variety show itself, Ian and Janette treated Mum and me and Janette's mum and dad, Bill and Mary Anderson, to a night at The Savoy. I remember the thrill of walking in the doors of the famous hotel, but it was nothing compared to the look on Bill's face. A former miner, he'd never even visited London before that day, never mind staying at The Savoy. The pride on Bill's face at what his wee girl had achieved will remain with me forever.

Bill and Mary were bewildered when they were shown into a room with no bed and admitted their confusion to Janette when she called from rehearsals to check they were comfortable. Janette asked if there was another door in the room and Mary told her there was but that she had assumed it was a connecting door to another room. She was astonished when she finally opened it and discovered the bedroom and toilet that made up the other half of their suite.

We were all so proud of Ian and Janette as we filed into the foyer of the Palladium and took our seats just four rows from the front. That year's show was attended by the Queen Mother and, just before the show began, there was a huge round of applause as she entered the royal box and sat down.

The show featured a mix of old-school entertainers, such as Arthur Askey, Harry Secombe and Charlie Drake, along with some younger (at the time) performers, such as Paul Daniels, Marti Caine and The Nolan Sisters.

My heart was thumping when Ian walked on stage. There was no announcement, so the audience had no idea who he was or what he was about to do. In the clubs, the act started with Jimmy interrupting Ian on stage by wandering through the audience asking, "Have you seen me mam?" It had them rolling in the aisle. If it was good enough for the Barrow in Furness Labour Club all those years ago, it was good enough for the London Palladium. So, Jimmy marched down the aisle in search of his missing mother.

Cue mayhem then laughter, as the audience realised it was all part of the act.

The six minutes went well but it was their naughty final gag that stole the show. In rehearsals, Lord Delfont had warned Ian that it was too risky for royal eyes and ears but Ian had assured him that cheeky Jimmy would get away with it.

Ian challenged Jimmy to prove how clever he was. "What's three and three?" he asked.

"Six," replied Jimmy, counting on his fingers.

"Don't use your fingers," Ian ordered. "What's four and four?"

Jimmy put his hands behind his back. "Eight," he answered.

"You're still using your fingers. Put your hands in your pockets," said Ian. "One last time. What's five and five?"

Jimmy thrust his hands into his shorts, smiled and announced, "Eleven!"

The joke took the roof off the Palladium and, with millions watching live on TV, turned The Krankies into instant stars.

After the show, we all partied through the night in Ian's suite back at the hotel. I had to catch the first shuttle from Heathrow to Glasgow in the morning, so I never actually went to bed, meaning I never did get to sleep at The Savoy.

I was now two months into my new role editing the *Weekly News* Irish sports pages, but it was only another five months before my career took another massive turn in a completely new direction.

By April 1979, someone obviously thought I was experiencing some sort of success as an editor, as I was asked to travel to DC Thomson's head office in Dundee for a two-week stint editing the paper's motoring and health pages. With no medical training and still unable to drive, I felt I was a strange choice for the job but happily packed my bags and boarded the train to the city of jute, jam and journalism, so called because of the three industries that had dominated the area's economy.

When I arrived at the company's Meadowside headquarters on my first Tuesday morning, it soon became obvious that far from filling in for a holiday vacancy, I was in Dundee on a trial period with the prospect of a long-term move to the company's flagship title almost assured.

Later that day, the editor, Bill Anderson, took me for lunch to the Royal Tay Yacht Club, where he was a member. Referred to by the entire staff as "Flash", but never to his face, he was a daunting figure with a small black moustache, who with a simple look could strike fear into the heart of even the most seasoned *Post* journalist.

The power of his gaze was frighteningly demonstrated on that day's 10-minute drive from Dundee city centre to the yacht club in Broughty Ferry, when a young boy almost ran out in front of him. Flash stopped the car, wound down the window and stared at the lad. Transfixed by his intense mesmeric glare, the boy just stood staring at Flash's face. Then without a word to either the boy or me, Flash wound the window back up and drove off.

Already daunted by the prospect of lunch with the editor of Scotland's best-selling newspaper, the grand surroundings of the yacht club, with its sparkling white tablecloths, did little to put me at ease.

As we sat down, Flash lit up a cigar and got straight to the point. He'd been editor of *The Post* for 10 years and, while he had no immediate plans to step down, he was beginning to think about his successor. At 19, I was the perfect age to take over from him in 10 years or so. I was astonished. This was not what I had expected at all.

We continued our lunch and Flash laid out the principles of what had made *The Post* Scotland's most successful newspaper. It was a masterclass in editing a newspaper or magazine, much of which over the next 40 years shaped the publications I edited.

He urged me to have a notional reader in my mind. In the case of *The Post*, he imagined a Mrs McGinty, and his advice to "Ask yourself, would Mrs McGinty be interested in that?" has always stuck with me.

One of the other key messages he gave me was, where possible, "rely on evolution not revolution". Most people would tell you *The Post* hadn't changed in decades, he said, but the truth was the paper changed a tiny amount every week, ensuring that readers never got bored but also were never frightened by major changes.

I got back to my Dundee hotel room that night both

excited and scared. On the one hand, this was a huge opportunity but on the other it appeared to place me on a 10-year journey through my 20s that would be dictated by DC Thomson and in which I would have little or no say.

The manner of my arrival at the Dundee office also had me worried. I'd been introduced to the office as the new boy up from Glasgow, at which point the journalist who was currently editing the health and motoring pages was informed, in front of the office, that I would be taking over his job. No quiet word before I arrived, just a very public elbowing aside. It shocked me and made me very wary.

Later that week, however, I got a call from Glasgow that was to offer me a completely different career path.


Since my days writing the school column, I'd become friendly with David Kelso, the young editor at my local paper, *The Clydebank Press*, often meeting up with him at Clydebank football matches. He contacted me in Dundee to tell me that the editor of the two other newspapers in his group, *The Govan Press* and *The Renfrew Press*, had left the company, and that the managing director was looking for a replacement.

By chance, the following week Clydebank were due to travel to Raith Rovers in Kirkcaldy, 25 miles south of Dundee, for a league game. So we made arrangements to see each other in the press box at the club's Stark's Park to talk about the job.

I made the 45-minute train journey from Dundee to the Fife town, and David travelled up from Clydebank for the meeting in the cylindrical cigar tube-shaped press box. It became obvious from the very start of our conversation that the two papers were not in a good state. The former editor had developed a drink problem that had let to standards – and sales – dwindling.

The newspapers were owned by a family firm, John

Cossar Ltd, and the Cossar printing press developed by the family was a mainstay of small newspapers across the British Empire around the start of the twentieth century. *The Govan Press* itself had celebrated its centenary the previous year, and *The Renfrew Press* was just a little younger. Unfortunately, it appeared that little had been done to modernise the papers in the intervening years and a rot had set in.

The project excited me greatly, however, and I asked David to put my name forward to the managing director, Harry McNab, as a potential editor.

I now had two very different potential career avenues…

The interview with Harry went well and it was clear that I would have carte blanche to do with the papers whatever I saw fit. The prospect thrilled me. When I got a call to offer me the job, I decided to take the chance and leave the safe confines of DC Thomson, where my future had been mapped out for me, and join a local newspaper group struggling for survival.

I had made up my mind that I wanted the job as I sat in my hotel room in Dundee, the night after my meeting in the Raith Rovers press box. Coincidentally, as I sat on my bed in the small attic room, the early results of the 1979 general election were being announced on the TV. It seemed that as my career took another turn, making me the country's youngest newspaper editor, the United Kingdom was in for a massive change of direction too, as Margaret Thatcher stepped onto the national stage.

# CHAPTER 6

It soon became obvious that there was more that required dumping at *The Govan Press* and *The Renfrew Press* than needed saving.

I had, however, been dealt a fortunate hand as far as staffing was concerned. My two reporters were a newly graduated journalism student from Napier College in Edinburgh and a trainee. While small in number, I had the luxury of not having to persuade an inherited staff that the drastic changes I planned were necessary.

The two papers served very different communities. Working-class Govan had been a standalone burgh – the fifth largest in Scotland – until it was swallowed up by the city of Glasgow in the early part of the twentieth century, but it remained staunchly independent. It had been the centre of the world-renowned Clydeside shipbuilding industry but by the late seventies the yards were struggling to survive and unemployment was rife.

Renfrew, on the other hand, was an altogether more-genteel area. The county town of Renfrewshire, it too had a history of shipbuilding but by the seventies boiler-maker Babock & Wilcox was a major employer in the town.

In a highly politicised area, I had no problems finding news for the Govan paper, but Renfrew was another story. It was a much more reserved community, reluctant to share its business with outsiders. So, when a few months into my editorship the trainee moved to our sister paper in Clydebank, I saw the opportunity to solve my problem.

Match reports for the local football team, Renfrew Juniors, were personally delivered to the office in Govan by a short, stout, bald, pipe-smoking man in his mid-50s called Bill Rew. He lived with his mother and enjoyed his visits to drop off his closely typed 200 words each week, during which he would share all the gossip that was circulating in Renfrew.

I decided Bill, who worked at Babcocks and had no journalistic experience other than his weekly football summaries, would be the perfect reporter for the paper. His prose left a lot to be desired, but that could easily be sorted at the editing stage. The important thing was he offered me a way into the town's activities.

Bill was astonished when I offered him the job. It was something he'd always dreamed of doing and, with no family ties other than his mother to look after, he accepted.

Sitting at his desk, portly Bill, pipe or tiny cheroot cigar dangling from his mouth, looked every bit the veteran local newsman. Newcomers to the office regularly turned to him as they entered, in search of the editor, only for him to point them in the direction of the acne-strewn teenager at the other end of the office.

With Bill's recruitment, I now had my team in place and was ready to transform the papers.

I decided the quickest way to signal that the newspapers were changing was to switch their headline fonts. The papers were set in a serif font. Serif is the small lines attached to letters – think of the Dior or HSBC logos, or the typeface most books use for text. The alternative is a san serif font – for example, the logos used by Microsoft or Google.

Serif typefaces can look authoritative, but they also suggest the weight of history. San serif offers a more-modern impression, which was what I desperately wanted to convey to signal that the papers were not a pair of expiring geriatrics but had something to offer a readership in the second half of the twentieth century.

I chose Helvetica to communicate modernity. It's the font that's used by BMW, Panasonic and Lufthansa, to name but a few, and I was happy that it positioned the papers as both contemporary and progressive.

Next, I wanted something that would attract younger readers, who I hoped would encourage their parents or grandparents to become regular purchasers.

When I was primary school age, my father's aunt Lesley used to collect her issues of *The People's Friend*, the women's magazine traditionally bought by an older generation of Scots, and present them to me when we visited so I could read the comic strips.

From my recent time at DC Thomson, I knew that *The Sunday Post*'s *Oor Willie* and *The Broons* strips had similar success attracting young readers, transforming it into a truly family newspaper. My ambition was to do something similar, but with virtually no budget how could I?

Little did I know that the answer to my problem was to involve me employing a writer the prestigious *New York Times* later described as, "one of several revered comics figures who, beginning in the late 1980s, dragged the medium into the modern day."

It began when a regular visitor to the office, community councillor Walter Morrison, walked through the door. Walter was very politically active in the Govan area and was a regular contributor to the Govan paper. On this occasion, he had brought in a portfolio of artwork drawn by his teenage son Grant. Grant had been featured three years before in a *Govan Press* article and Walter wanted to know if I was interested in running a follow-up.

Walter showed me the first story, which had told how 16-year-old Grant's interest in comic books had led him and a couple of school friends to develop their own superhero characters. When he showed me Grant's drawings, I was impressed and asked Grant to pop into the office for a chat. Just three months younger than me, he was a shy lad but became energised when we began talking about comic books, and he loved the idea of creating a Clydeside-based superhero.

I suggested the name *Captain Clyde*, as Captain America was a huge hit for Marvel comics in the sixties and seventies and I liked the alliteration.

In his 2011 autobiography, *Supergods*, Grant confessed, "My friends and I thought the name was only slightly less pathetic than the kind of music our dads like, but I'd already decided to redeem it by taking a new and more believable approach to the material, giving the stereotypical title an ironic kick."

It's fair to say, reading Grant's comments in *Supergods*, I believe his impression was that I was out of touch with where comic books were heading and that I encouraged a "camp" Batman TV series-style approach because of that. My concept for the character, however, was based on what I felt was right for the readers of the papers, who, given the advancing age of many of them, I knew would have trouble with a superhero comic strip of any kind, never mind one with an offbeat edge.

We agreed a very small £6-a-week fee for the weekly episodes – the equivalent of four two-litre bottles of Coca-Cola – and I reserved half a page a week for the strip. As well as *The Govan Press and Renfrew Press*, it would also run in the titles' sister publication *The Clydebank Press*.

Grant created an alter ego for his hero – unemployed Glaswegian Chris Neville, whose speech was scattered with West of Scotland colloquialisms. While hill walking on holiday in the English Peak District, something Grant had done the previous summer, Chris happened upon the pagan "Goddess of the Earth Energy", who had entrusted him with superpowers.

Captain Clyde's first adventure cleverly embraced a topical local news story. The Glasgow Underground system had recently been renovated but the reopening date had been postponed, with no reason being given for the hold up.

Grant's story proposed that the delay had been caused by a horde of alien monsters discovered under the Tube station at Govan, and Captain Clyde stepped in to save the city. Next, he introduced a supervillain, named Quasar, and the strip was up and running.

As Grant himself admits in *Supergods*, as time went on, "the stories turned darker and quirkier", while Chris' girlfriend, Alison, "blossomed from mousy student to styled sex kitten in high heels and tight jeans". The themes became more and more adult, and escapism turned to horror. The strip began to part company from my readership.

After nearly three years and more than 150 episodes, I decided that *Captain Clyde* had gone as far as it could – possibly further than he should have! – and Grant had probably outgrown the papers too.

One day, a salesman for US syndication giant King Features appeared at my door. "How much do you pay for *Captain Clyde?*" he asked.

I told him.

"I can offer you half a page a week of *Tom and Jerry* for the same money," he guaranteed.

The deal was done, the TV cat-and-mouse duo joined the papers, and Grant and I went our separate ways.

Grant credits his growth as a writer in those early years to his 150 episodes of *Captain Clyde* saying, "The discipline had improved my artwork and storytelling to a much more professional standard."

He went on to find fame, and an MBE, as one of the most sought-after comic book writers of the late twentieth and early twenty-first century, regenerating classic heroes, from Batman, Superman and Wonder Woman to X-Men and the Justice League of America. He later adapted his graphic novel *Happy!* for television before overseeing the 2020 TV adaptation of Aldous Huxley's *Brave New World*.

As a teenager submitting his weekly artwork on A3 paper, he always added a small "copyright Morrison" mark in the bottom right-hand side of the sheet. At the time it seemed somewhat pretentious but looking back, Grant obviously knew he was destined for success.

Coincidentally, the creator of another hit TV superhero also regularly visited me at the cramped Govan office in those days.

On one of my first days on the job, an ineffectual man in a bunnet, a Scottish flat cap, turned up at the office, introduced himself as the papers' crossword compiler and explained he'd driven up from Ayrshire to deliver a batch of puzzles for upcoming issues.

As we made conversation, he mentioned he'd just had a children's book published and he was in discussions with a broadcaster about turning it into a big-budget TV series. I'm embarrassed to say that after he left my office I suggested to the team that there was more than a little wishful thinking in his talk of a TV series.

It was a shock then, when a few years later Forrest Wilson's *Supergran* books were adapted for television, with a catchy theme song sung by comedian Billy Connolly, a turn of events that taught me never to judge a book, or its author, by its cover.

The third phase of my plan for the papers was to embed them deeper into the political landscape of the areas, particularly in Govan which had a rich history of political activism.

As luck would have it, a new local MP, Andy McMahon, had been elected to the Govan constituency in the May 1979 General Election, just weeks before I took over the papers, and he was very keen on raising his profile with his new constituents.

Andy, a former Communist Party member, had become the Labour candidate for the Govan seat simply because it was his turn. That was the way Labour politics worked in Glasgow in the seventies. He had served his time as a local councillor and had reached the point in the pecking order where he was the natural successor to the previous MP, Harry Selby.

Andy spent much of his time in office signed off ill by his GP, however, so he rarely visited the Palace of Westminster, making it even more important that he kept up his profile with the Govan voters.

It was a match made in heaven – a new young editor in search of strong political stories and a politician in need of a mouthpiece. Looking back, I can't say that I'm proud of the unholy unspoken alliance we formed, but at the time it seemed the perfect union.

It worked like this…

Andy would call the paper to point out that a constituent had complained that the streetlights in a certain street hadn't been working for a week. We would call the corporation lighting department, they would fix the lights, and Andy would comment in the next week's paper, as if the success was due to him.

On other occasions, Andy would simply comment on the latest Conservative government initiative. It filled column inches in *The Press* and his views were in tune with the vast majority of our working-class readership.

It was a convention that was to lead to an embarrassing incident that I feared at the time would lead to the end of my short career.

Ewan Watt, my "senior" reporter, later in his career became chief sub-editor at *The Sun* and assistant editor of Scotland's best-selling paper, the *Daily Record*. But at the time he was fresh out of journalism college and, like me, a teenager.

Our shared teenage sense of humour led to Ewan inserting what we both considered amusing comments in the stories he wrote. When the typed story arrived on my desk, I'd delete the comments with my pen as part of the editing process before sending the words through to the typesetter.

Andy would regularly call me on a Friday morning when his paper had been delivered and we'd discuss the contents. When the phone rang on this particular Friday, Andy sounded less jovial than I had come to expect.

"Hello, Colin? It's Andy McMahon here," he said.

"Andy, how are things with you," I answered cheerfully.

"Not too good," he replied. "It's the piece in this week's *Press* about my wife being frigid."

I froze. "Sorry, Andy, can you repeat that?" I asked, frantically waving my arms at Ewan to bring me a copy of that week's issue.

"The article on page 3," he continued, "that mentions my wife..." His voice trailed off.

I frantically turned to page 3 and a story in which Andy had commented about government plans to alter the way unemployment benefit was paid. My eyes desperately scanned each line of the article until I read the last lines of Andy's quote – "...attending the offices each week means there are smaller queues and less frustration (unless your wife happens to be frigid)."

I was horrified but Andy carried on talking. "You know I can see the funny side of it, but my friends are saying—"

I cut him off. "No, no, Andy, it's not funny at all. I'm so sorry, it must have been one of the printers that added it in," I claimed. The printers were a common scapegoat for many mistakes.

Andy was still talking, however. "Well, it's just that my wife's not been well recently, so I wondered if you could just put a piece in next week's edition saying that..."

I cut in before he could complete the sentence. "That your wife's not frigid?" I asked, astonished at what I was hearing.

"Aye, that would help,' he suggested.

I was caught in a nightmare. I thought about suggesting to him that the story was so dull, few readers would have lasted until the offending line, but that might only have added fuel to the fire. I did, however, manage to talk him out of a printed correction and by the following Monday he was once again cheerfully calling me to suggest a story we might want to cover.

That weekend, I decided to keep quiet about the offensive passage and hoped no one would reach that point in the soporific article, especially my boss, Harry McNab.

Luckily, my hunch was correct and the blunder went undetected. Many months later, towards the end of an alcohol-fuelled lunch, I admitted my embarrassing cock up to Harry, who had been a journalist himself before becoming managing director.

"Well, Mr Tough," said a rosy-cheeked Harry, a man I respected greatly, "I think you have learnt a huge lesson and I suspect you will never forget it."

He was right, the worry the incident caused stayed with me throughout my career and was referenced time and time again when explaining to journalists and designers why you should never fool about with live copy.

It wasn't the only occasion in which my youthful exuberance got me into trouble. A story Bill brought to me about a Chinese delegation visiting the local Rolls Royce factory, which I splashed across the front page with the headline "Chinese invade Renfrew", brought complaints from both the car manufacturer and the Chinese embassy.

Thankfully, there were more triumphs than disasters as we set about the rehabilitation of the papers.

I decided it was important that the publications embraced and supported the local community, rather than simply report what was taking place. So, when I heard the story of a young Govan girl called Lesley McColl, whose family was attempting to raise £8000 to send her to Philadelphia for medical treatment, it seemed the perfect way to help a good cause and to promote the paper.

Little Lesley was eight and had learning difficulties, and the clinic in the States offered her the hope of finding a cure for an illness that had baffled experts on both sides of the Atlantic. I explained in a front-page story that this was the chance "for the people of the Govan area to show they have the generosity and kindness to help a little girl who has been dealt a cruel blow so early in her life".

As so often is the case in socially deprived areas, the people of the area rose to the challenge and the money rolled in. It was an achievement I was proud of and one that helped to raise the paper's profile.

Buoyed by the success of the campaign, when local residents came to me asking for help with another fight, I was eager to get *The Press* involved.

Govan was home to Scottish footballing giants Rangers, and in 1971 they opened the Rangers Social Club. It was the biggest cabaret club of its kind in Scotland, with a capacity of 450. Stars such as Lulu, The Drifters and Bob Monkhouse featured on the bill and for a few years it was a huge success, but by the time I was editing the *Govan Press*, eight years later, its glory days were a distant memory.

Eric Morley, who ran the Miss World beauty competition, an annual pageant shown on BBC1, was attempting to buy the club, and the local residents were unhappy about the prospect. As usual, Andy McMahon was happy to supply a quote supporting his constituents. "We'll have sex clubs in Govan next," was his inflammatory prediction.

It was too good to be true. "Sex clubs for Govan" read the huge banner headline across the front of that week's paper, illustrating that internet click-bait had been a staple of newspapers long before the days of the *Mail Online*. Sales soared that week.

The crusade won a regular weekly place in the columns of the paper, and its supporters became frequent visitors to the *Press* office.

Eventually, the fight was lost and the grand opening of "Morley's Nite Spot" – the spelling of "Nite" adding seventies sophistication to the establishment it was believed – was scheduled.

Soon after, tickets to the star-studded occasion arrived at the office for Ewan, me and partners. It was billed as Glasgow's social event of the year, and for two 19-year-old boys it was a huge thrill. Ewan took his soon-to-be wife, Michelle, and I took my girlfriend, Hazel.

There was huge excitement inside our taxi as we arrived at the nightclub, to be met by an immaculately dressed doorman, who opened the car door with a flourish. As the four of us stepped out of the Mercedes, however, we were met by a wall of noise, as the protesters who had become regulars in our office until only a few weeks before, shouted and jeered at the arriving celebrities and dignitaries.

Heads down, we darted round the back of the car and quickly sped up the stairs of the club to meet the reception committee, which included Morley, his wife, the Lord Provost of Glasgow and Miss World. Naive teenagers that we were, it hadn't even struck us that although the campaign had been lost, the protesters might still feel the need to demonstrate at the launch. Luckily, we made it inside without being spotted; otherwise the credibility we had worked so hard to develop would have been in tatters.

Rangers weren't Govan's only football club. The burgh

played host to two other teams, Benburb and St Anthony's, both of which were non-league Junior clubs. While Rangers had a huge international following, I knew from my dad's involvement in Junior football what clubs like these meant to their local communities.

So when Benburb reached the Scottish Junior Cup final at Hampden Park, I wanted to do something special in the paper. In the sixties and seventies, the Glasgow *Evening Times* produced weekly colour wrap-arounds with their early evening Saturday editions – with poster-size photos of Rangers players when the club was playing at home and Celtic when they had home advantage.

I decided that a colour shot of the Benburb team wrapped around the normal paper on cup final week would be the perfect souvenir for fans, and that as well as being sold in the normal local newsagents, copies could be sold outside Hampden.

*The Govan Press* had celebrated its 100th birthday just two years before and in all that time it had never carried a colour photo. I was thrilled at the prospect of the team pic dominating the front and back of the issue.

The colour pages had to be printed on a thicker paper stock at another printer and transported to the Govan presses to be wrapped around each issue. The presses ran all night, and I relished spending the wee small hours inhaling the sooty aroma of the newsprint. By morning, it was ready to go on sale. It was one of my proudest moments as I took my seat in the Hampden press box and handed out copies of the souvenir colour special to colleagues I had worked with a few years earlier as a sports reporter.

As I said before, Govan was an amazingly politically active area. Six years earlier, Scottish National Party candidate Margo MacDonald had sent shock waves through British politics by winning the Govan by-election for the SNP, only the fourth parliamentary victory in the party's history but an early warning to Labour that its support was on the rise.

Andy McMahon's predecessor as MP, Harry Selby, won the seat back at the next general election but 15 years later, in 1988, Jim Sillar's win for the Nationalists was even more seismic and marked the first tremors of the earthquake that was to lead to the party's dominance of Scottish politics.

For most of the twentieth century, however, Govan was firmly part of Red Clydeside, from the rent strikes in the early years through to the Upper Clyde Shipbuilders Work-In of the seventies, and the Labour Party and Communist Party dominated the political landscape.

It wasn't surprising then that one of the roles I found myself asked to fulfil as the local newspaper editor was chairman of an election debate. The event was held in a Govan school hall, and the seats and tables were configured on stage in a layout similar to TV's *Question Time*.

Coincidentally, the son of a Clydebank Church of Scotland clergyman was one of the candidates. Iain Lawson's father, the Rev Dr Alex Lawson, was in fact, the minister at Kilbowie Church, the place of worship attended by my mother and where my father and his brother had been elders until both fell out with Lawson.

Following my father's death, Alex Lawson had come to pay respects to my mum, only to become involved in a religious argument with me. I considered Lawson's beliefs to be bigoted and, grief stricken by my dad's death, I was in no mood to listen to his sickening view of the world. Something snapped in me and, much to my mother's embarrassment, I demanded he leave the house.

Iain, on the other hand, was a likeable young man in his late-20s, at the time. He was the Conservative Party candidate, although he was later to join the SNP and hold several senior positions in the party.

The election debate got underway and, sitting hunched over my notes, with a squadron of butterflies in my stomach, a dry mouth and a shaky voice, I introduced the candidates one by one.

As the evening went on, the nerves melted away and my confidence soared. I began to unravel my body and lean back in my chair. I swung round from candidate to candidate, pointing at them as I challenged them to answer a point made by an opponent. I was quite good at this hosting lark, I smugly thought to myself. As each question was directed to the team, I quickly précised the question for clarity.

"OK, last question of the night. The gentleman over here," I confidently announced as the evening was drawing to a close, pointing to a man sitting next to Grant Morrison's father, Walter. I felt assured that any friend of Walter's would have a strong political question to ask.

As the man began to speak, however, my assurance evaporated as it became obvious he had a serious motor neuron disease that affected his speech. His point was complex, lasting what felt like several minutes, and his entire question was incomprehensible.

The blood was pounding in my ears, I began sweating, my mouth was once again as dry as a Govan Shipbuilder's graving dock, and, as he ended his question, I felt the eyes of the audience drilling into my face.

I took the coward's way out and, unable to summarise the question, I skipped the précis I'd been delivering to previous questions and turned to the candidates. "So," I said, scrambling for words, "who wants to start us on this question."

The candidates now also looked petrified, as their eyes darted from one to the other.

With, understandably, no taker, I was required to choose one of the panellists to face the question. Poor Iain Lawson.

His father's prejudice and arrogance at the time of my own dad's death, beliefs I had no reason to think Iain shared, put him straight into the firing line.

"Iain, would you like to give us your thoughts on this one, please?"

As the colour drained from his face, a voice in the audience shouted out, "I'm afraid my friend may have been a little difficult to hear."

Walter Morrison went on to repeat the question concisely. It was a kind gesture, as Walter's politics were at the other end of the political spectrum from Iain's, and it would have been very easy to have watched him sit in embarrassed silence.

# CHAPTER 7

Things had gone well in the short time I'd been in charge of the two papers, so when the editor of the company's flagship title, my own local newspaper, *The Clydebank Press*, resigned to join Scotland's best-selling daily newspaper, the *Daily Record*, I was asked to take the editor's chair.

It was strange to find myself in charge of the newspaper I'd read since childhood and which so often had carried reports of my own father's exploits as a local councillor.

Again, I set out to modernise the paper, although it needed far less work than the Renfrew and Govan publications.

I swept up all the district court stories that were scattered around the paper and introduced a dedicated section. Many readers would buy the paper to gloat at their neighbours' court appearances, often for minor offences such as being drunk and disorderly or urinating in a public place, knowing full well that a member of their own family was likely to be facing similar charges in the coming weeks. On the other hand, I also knew some readers found this side of Clydebank society distasteful and to be avoided, so I concluded that by offering a section that readers could either make a beeline to, or completely ignore, suited both sets of readers.

I also added a feature I'd first introduced in the Govan paper that dedicated a page to a Q&A with local movers and shakers – from priests and ministers to headmasters and politicians.

Coincidentally, just weeks after I took over the job I found myself invited to a weekly meeting with the great and the good of the town, leading to a rather embarrassing incident.

When I took over the editorship of *The Clydebank Press*, the area had the highest unemployment rate in Europe. For almost a hundred years, the workforce of the town had largely been employed by two businesses – shipbuilder John Brown and the Singer sewing machine factory.

John Brown had built some of the world's greatest liners, from the *Lusitania* and the *Empress of Britain* to the three Queens, the *Queen Mary*, the *Queen Elizabeth* and the *QE2*, along with numerous battleships and the royal yacht *Britannia*.

The people of the town were rightfully proud of what the term "Clyde-built" meant in the world, and the success of the town's other exports, its sewing machines, also instilled a sense of self-respect in the close-knit community.

The sewing machine factory was huge, employing at its height more than 11,500 Bankies and producing 80 per cent of the world's sewing machines, a must-have gadget in the first half of the twentieth century. Such was the community's dependence on the factory that a sewing machine was incorporated into the town's coat of arms. In my travels around the world, I've seen Clydebank Singer sewing machines in all kinds of strange places, including a remote village in the jungles of Cambodia.

Everything about the factory was on a huge scale. With nearly one million feet of space, it was served by its own railway station on the Helensburgh-to-Glasgow line. The face of the factory clock, which stood on a tower 200-feet tall and which the burgh used to tell the time, was five feet larger than London's Big Ben.

Entire families worked there, including my own relatives and neighbours. Then in 1980, the factory closed. That same year, oil rig manufacturer Marathon sold the John Brown shipyard it had bought in the early seventies, when John Brown's shipyard had ceased to exist and the business had switched to building drilling platforms for the North

Sea. The change of ownership led to further job losses for a yard that had been haemorrhaging jobs throughout the seventies, leaving the town of 50,000 with a horrendous unemployment rate of more than one in five adults.

So it was that the Clydebank Campaign on Employment was set up in the late seventies, made up of the area's politicians, including the town's provost, the Scottish equivalent of the mayor, clergymen, headmasters, police and fire representatives and the like. As the local newspaper editor, I was invited to join.

The first meeting I attended was held at the house of a local priest, Father Jimmy McShane. I hadn't met Jimmy before and, although I knew a number of the other representatives, I was apprehensive as I rang the doorbell beside his glass-panelled front door. He met me with a cheery "hello" and showed me into his dining room where the other members of the campaign had begun to meet.

At just 20, I was the youngest member of the group by more than 20 years, and I couldn't help feeling a large degree of what would now be described as impostor syndrome – the internal experience of believing that you are not as competent as others perceive you to be.

Soon, a dozen of us were sitting around a table taking up most of the room, leaving barely enough space to move around the periphery without being forced to breathe in.

Putting everyone at ease, as I later discovered was his skill, Jimmy asked, "What's everyone having to drink?", looking directly at me first and raising his eyebrows in a questioning manner.

Nervous about my new companions and my new status as a town-worthy, Jimmy's kind offer of a drink made the moment feel much more like a social occasion and went some way to putting me at ease.

"I'll have a gin and tonic please, Jimmy." I smiled back at him.

"Provost?" Jimmy asked.

"Orange juice, please," Provost McKendrick said, followed by a request for a Coke, a mineral water, another Coke, and so on, until the entire table had given their preferences, with only the young newspaper editor having taken the alcoholic option at this mid-afternoon meeting.

My embarrassment grew as Jimmy handed me the highball glass, topped with ice and a slice of lemon. But, much to my relief, he saved me from total mortification by taking the gin bottle in his hand, sitting down next to me and proclaiming, "Well, looks like it's just you and me then," as he poured himself a sizeable measure and raised it to the room.

I doubt very much if under normal circumstances, Jimmy would have poured himself a gin. It was, I'm pretty sure, a kind act to save face for an inexperienced young journalist, and I was incredibly grateful.

Clydebank's proud industrial history played a major part in my favourite *Clydebank Press* editorial a couple of years later. Neither *The Renfrew* nor *The Govan Press* had carried an editorial, the opinion piece where traditionally the editor gives a personal view on the issues of the day.

Clydebank, like Govan, had always been an extremely politically active area. When my father was first elected to the council, the Labour Party dominated the town and the official opposition was the Communist Party. Dad stood under the banner of the Independent Ratepayers Association, a group he helped found in the fifties on a platform that included keeping party politics out of local government and improving housing, transport and shopping facilities.

Even in a town with such a strong political heritage, coming up with a new slant for an editorial every week was a draining business. Every once in a while, though, an event would lend itself to celebration or condemnation, and the Falklands War provided one such moment.

When Argentina, led by their military leader General Galtieri, invaded the Falklands in 1982, Prime Minister Margaret Thatcher sent a naval task force of 127 ships packed with British military troops to regain the islands. It's impossible to explain how quickly Britain's attitude changed following the invasion.

A peace-loving population in March became a hawkish nation by April. The public unanimously supported a war with Argentina, and a mood of jingoistic sabre-rattling overtook the bulk of the country's population.

Stores displayed signs reading "We do not sell Argentine corned beef", with plastic packets of sliced beef removed from shelves and the only cans in sight displaying labels reading "Made in Brazil". Argentina football stars, such as 1978 World Cup winner Ossie Ardiles, who played for Spurs, were booed, and Ossie eventually felt forced to leave England and go on loan to Paris.

At the time, Ian and Janette were at the height of their post-Royal Variety success, taking their Krankies theatre show around the country. Before the tour began, the war with Argentina had broken out and, unfortunately, they had engaged an Argentinian who performed a gaucho act with swinging bolas, the traditional Argentinian weapon involving weights on the ends of interconnected ropes, used to capture animals by entangling their legs.

An awkward feeling of latent hostility came over the audience as the poor performer walked on stage on the show's opening night. However, he had a cunning plan. He explained he was going to knock a cigarette out of his girl assistant's mouth with the swinging bolas, but first he would practise with a polystyrene head. His assistant held the head at arm's length and popped the cigarette in its mouth.

The gaucho began spinning his bolas and, to build

tension for his attempt with the assistant, his normal act involved him missing the cigarette and smashing the bolas into the plastic head.

He swung the rope, the bolas clattered into the head, and he turned to the audience and declared, "General Galtieri." The crowd screamed, he had them on his side and the act became an instant hit. Off stage, however, he still argued with Ian that the islands belonged to Argentina.

With that amount of national backing for the war, therefore, when it was announced that the *QE2* was to act as a troop carrier to make the journey to the south Atlantic, it seemed the obvious topic for an editorial.

Under the heading "Pride of a town", I wrote:

*The pride of the working men of Clydebank will sail shortly to face the unknown hazards of the South Atlantic.*

*The "Queen Elizabeth II" launched at the town's John Brown Shipyard, has been requisitioned by the Ministry of Defence to join the Task Force.*

*The ship will carry more than 3,000 brave British soldiers to the icy waters around the Falkland Islands.*

*For many Clydebank men the launching of the QEII was the proudest moment of their lives.*

*They had stamped their identity on every rivet, bolt and screw and they were justifiably proud of the end result.*

*The ship's speed and facilities, so prized by the Ministry of Defence, owe much to the workmanship of the town.*

*As she sails to the war zone, the pride and spirit of Clydebank goes with her.*

*Godspeed.*

The reaction from the people of the town was amazing, with men stopping in the street to offer their thanks and tell me that the words brought tears to their eyes. The editorial, however, had a polarising effect on members of the Labour council. While some saw the words as the tribute it was meant to be, others, following the national party's stance, were critical of any support for the war.

Coincidentally, the year before the Falklands conflict, I'd spent a couple of weeks with the Air Defence Division, which later was to play a major role in winning the war.

The Ministry of Defence had invited me to Dortmund to meet some of the local Clydebank soldiers serving in Germany. Deprived working-class areas like Clydebank had long been fertile recruiting grounds for the British forces, and trips by the local paper provided good stories for the Press and a good way for the military to enlist recruits.

Six months after Dortmund, I was invited to follow up the visit with a trip to Benbecula, the rocky wind-swept Outer Hebridean island with a civilian population of fewer than 1500, where the regiment held manoeuvres.

As I sat on the beach at the controls of the giant Rapier surface-to-air missiles, I was puzzled as to why the army was training its soldiers on a rocky outcrop in the Atlantic when, with the Cold War still at its height, the threat to British forces came from Russia along the border of East and West Germany. Little did I, or the army, know at the time that within a few months another rocky outcrop in the Atlantic, although south of the equator rather than north, would provide the location for a theatre of war.


My time as editor of the three Scottish local newspapers coincided with Ian and Janette taking over as hosts of the iconic BBC TV children's series *Crackerjack*. The show was a huge hit when I was a child, when it starred comedians Leslie Crowther and Peter Glaze.

The disembodied voice announcing, "It's Friday... it's five to five... it's Crackerjack!", and the kids in the audience joining in to bawl the title of the programme, marked the start of the weekend for British school children throughout the sixties, seventies and eighties.

Peter Glaze was still starring in the show in the late seventies, along with comic Bernie Clifton, despite the fact that Peter was by that time in his 60s, so the BBC decided that the series needed a new, younger team. Following the success of The Krankies at the Royal Variety, they offered Ian and Janette the gig, along with Lancashire comedian Stu Francis.

Ian and Janette were now household names across the UK and hugely popular with both adults and children, but during the first few weeks of the new series they both felt something was lacking from their performance. The reaction they were receiving from the audience in the Shepherd's Bush Television Theatre, where the programme was recorded, just wasn't what they'd come to expect in theatres and clubs.

Ian asked to see Robin Nash, the head of BBC Variety, which produced the show, to discuss the problem. Nash was what is often described as "Old school BBC", a flamboyant former wing commander in the Royal Air Force with a moustache and bow tie. As they discussed the theatre audience's reaction, Ian asked where the children were sourced from, and it turned out that they were mostly from public schools.

Ian asked, "Why don't you get some working-class kids from the local area around Shepherd's Bush?"

His suggestion was met by Nash with a wrinkled nose, and the assertion, "We tried that and they were much too disruptive."

Ian knew, however, that what was needed was a noisy, raucous audience that would produce an exciting atmosphere for the viewers at home, so he insisted that local children should be invited to join the audience. The new audience, which now included Black and Asian children for

110

the first time, had the desired effect, the atmosphere improved and the viewing figures began to grow, climbing from 2.5 million to 9.5 million in just two years.

I was 20, single and living at home when Ian and Janette took over *Crackerjack*. The money I was making as a newspaper editor allowed me to travel down to London on a regular basis and visit them, sleeping on the couch in their flat at Oxford and Cambridge Mansions in Marylebone.

I enjoyed attending the recordings of the series in Shepherd's Bush, but even better were the nights out in London's West End, with a regular late-night venue being a club called Stringfellows – at the time, *the* place to be seen in the capital.

Stringfellows bore the name of the owner, Peter Stringfellow, a Sheffield businessman who had created a huge cabaret venue in the Yorkshire city where Ian and Janette had played regularly. Following success with clubs in his hometown and across the Pennines in Manchester, Stringfellow had opened the eponymous London club in 1980 and it had been an immediate success. Attracting national and international celebrities, from film and TV stars and rock musicians to footballers and models, it was constantly featured in the gossip pages of the tabloids.

I remember the thrill the first night I visited Stringfellows with Ian and Janette. We stepped out of our black cab with Stu, and out of the darkness were met with a barrage of flashing bulbs as the paparazzi took aim with their cameras.

As we moved towards the head of the huge queue snaking around the block, the bouncers politely lifted the rope used to keep the line in order and let us in the main door, where the noise, the smoke, the light and the heat hit us instantly.

Ian and Janette had just finished recording that Friday's episode of the show, which featured Bryan Robson, the Manchester United and England captain, as a guest, and he had joined us for our night out.

As we entered the room, the comedian Jim Davidson shouted over. I hadn't seen Jim since Ian and Janette had appeared in a pantomime with him in Bristol the year before, and he rushed over, slapping me on the back and hugging me.

Next, Eric Zee, a camp, bouffanted magician who performed an amazing stage act with a real leopard, hurried towards me. I'd met Eric on a number of occasions earlier in the year when he was touring theatres with Ian and Janette in a glamorous cabaret-style show called Palm Beach Review. He too greeted me enthusiastically and theatrically and I felt like I was the centre of attention.

Word began to get around that Bryan Robson was in the club. As our group pushed past Julian Lennon, Beatle John's son, to reach the bar, an inebriated reveller looking straight at the England skipper asked, "Which one of you lot is Bryan Robson?"

Without missing a beat, Bryan turned and pointed to me. "That's him there!" he assured him.

The customer, obviously not a football fan, grabbed me by the hand, pumping my arm up and down, excited to have met an England football legend. I'm certain it's an encounter that he's told many people about over the years. Unfortunately, it was an era before mobile phones. Otherwise I'm sure he would have requested a selfie, only to discover when he shared it online that he wasn't shaking hands with Bryan Robson, and that the football star was in fact the out-of-focus figure in the background ordering drinks.

Generally, however, I was almost invisible to other celebrities as I sat with Ian and Janette in Stringfellows. It mattered not one jot to me; at 20, I was just happy to be part of the coolest scene in London. Curly-permed Stringfellow himself would work the tables, moving from celebrity to celebrity, always with a huge smile on his face.

On one occasion, however, I found myself to be the centre of attention, with a table of stars hanging on my every word, and it said much about the power of celebrity.

A couple of weeks before that night, as editor of the Clydebank Press, I'd been invited to a church gathering. It was something that happened regularly when a local faith group had a visiting speaker who they felt might be of interest to the paper's readers, but it wasn't the type of event that I tended to commit a reporter to attend. This preacher, however, had such an exceptional story to tell that I accepted the invitation personally.

I was 10 when Neil Armstrong took his first steps on the moon, the perfect age to be caught up in the excitement of the greatest adventure story of the twentieth century. I owned a record album called *Journey to the Moon*, which on one side had recordings of the Gemini astronauts' early space missions and on the other, audio of the Apollo 11 moonshot. I had listened to the Cape Kennedy countdown and the moon-landing dialogue regularly on my small Dansette record player.

I had Airfix models of the Saturn V rocket and the moon lander that my dad and I had glued together, the commemorative issue of *TV Times* with Neil Armstrong on the cover, books about the mission... You name it, I owned it. Which was why, as I made my way to the church, I was thrilled to be meeting Jim Irwin, one of only 12 men in the world to have ever walked on the surface of the moon.

My deputy editor, Ewan, and I climbed the creaking spiral wooden staircase up to the church's balcony and sat in the front row, breathing in the dank musty scent of a gallery rarely used but packed for this prestigious guest.

Jim had been one of 19 astronauts chosen for the moon missions in 1966. He was the pilot of the Apollo 15 lunar module that he landed on the moon in July 1971, just two years after Armstrong's historic first visit to the moon. And he became the first automobile passenger on the moon when he accompanied his crewmate David Scott as he drove the first Lunar Roving Vehicle. Most significantly, the pair brought back to Earth the four-billion-year-old Genesis Rock, the oldest rock found in the universe.

After his return from space, Jim became a born-again Christian and founded the High Flight Foundation, spending 20 years travelling the world as a "Goodwill Ambassador for the Prince of Peace", stating that "Jesus walking on the Earth is more important than man walking on the moon". It was as part of his religious mission that he was visiting Clydebank.

I listened to his presentation in awe, hanging on his every word, and was particularly excited when he held up a rock that he claimed to have brought from the moon. Knowing I was to interview him directly after he ended his speech, I was thrilled at the possibility that I would be able to touch a moon rock. Alas, he admitted towards the end of his lecture that the rock he had with him was in fact a replica and that he had simply given the impression it was lunar in ancestry to make a philosophical point.

The disappointment in learning the moon rock was a fake was greatly outweighed by the fact that I was meeting one of the world's greatest heroes. Ewan and I bundled into a small room in the hall attached to the church, which had been set aside for the chat with Jim, and over a cup of tea we discussed his career as an astronaut and his trip to the moon.

It was obvious the mission had served as an epiphany to Jim. As he chatted, he explained how his view of the Earth from the lunar surface had affected his life.

"That beautiful, warm living object looked so fragile, so delicate, that if you touched it with a finger it would crumble and fall apart," he said. "Seeing this has to change a man."

To hear first-hand the testimony of a man who had experienced the most unique views in history was thrilling and humbling.

It was Jim's subsequent comments about what he didn't see on the moon that shocked me and Ewan. Having extolled the beauty of the vista that he had encountered, Jim suddenly switched to a more serious mood as he assured us, "I want you to know, there is no truth in the claims that we discovered alien structures on the moon."

Ewan and I looked at each other, puzzled by the astronaut's sudden change of tone and his denial of claims we weren't aware of and which he himself had introduced into the conversation. He excitedly explained there was no truth in stories that had been circulating – that during their lunar drive, he and Scott had come across a UFO and that the discovery had been covered up by NASA.

The vehemence of his argument and his determination to force it into the interview hit both me and Ewan as being totally out of context with the rest of the friendly chat, and it struck both of us as a case of the lady doth protest too much.

Whatever he did or didn't see on the moon, and in the internet age there's now plenty of conspiracy theorists happy to offer their opinions, Jim was a fascinating man with amazing stories to tell, including tales of his expeditions to Mount Ararat in Turkey to find Noah's Ark.

So, it was my encounter with Jim that resulted in my holding court to a table full of celebrities in Stringfellows that night in 1981. Around the table were me, Ian and Janette, Stringfellow himself, *The New Avengers'* Gareth Hunt, Diane Keen, star of the sitcom *The Cuckoo Waltz*, and a number of other names lost to me in the mists of time.

The topic of space travel had come up in the conversation and I'd mentioned that a couple of weeks previously I'd had a chat with one of the moon-landing astronauts. Suddenly, all eyes were on me as I related his feelings on seeing the Earth from space and his strange denial of having had an alien encounter.

In his biography, *The Fry Chronicles*, Stephen Fry illustrates how fame has its own pecking order with a story about sitting with Russell Harty, Alan Bennett and Alan Bates in Joe Allen's, the London American diner-style restaurant that's a favourite with actors, dancers, agents and producers. All eyes were on his table, "until suddenly heads swung towards the door. Laurence Olivier and Dustin Hoffman walked in. Our table no longer existed," he recalls.

In the Top Trumps of fame, it appeared that meeting an astronaut who had walked on the moon provided me with enough celebrity by association to momentarily trump the genuine celebs around the table.

I have a footnote to the story that concerns Gareth Hunt. As I said, a couple of years before the events of that evening, he had been the action hero Mike Gambit in the ITV series *The New Avengers*, alongside Joanna Lumley in her breakthrough role as Purdey, and Patrick McNee, as the suave John Steed. Around the early eighties, he was starring in a popular series of Nescafe coffee ads that kept him firmly in the public eye.

I remember him being a quite-unpleasant drunk and not someone whose company I particularly enjoyed. Fame, as it often does, had corrupted him into believing he was in some way superior to others. It was strange then that when I next met him a number of years later, when Ian and Janette worked with him in pantomime, he was a reformed character and a charming guy, who I almost went into business with – but that's a story for later.

Jim Irwin's UFO story continues to fascinate me. While still living at home in Clydebank, in my early 20s, I had an inexplicable close encounter myself. I was returning from an evening out in Glasgow one night when, stepping out of the taxi, I looked up at the sky and saw what appeared to be a huge object streak across the dark sky in seconds.

I asked the cab driver if he'd seen anything, but he had no idea what I was talking about. I was so surprised by the vision I'd seen that I called Glasgow Airport to report it. After a few minutes, I was transferred to a centre at Prestwick Airport that appeared to deal with similar sightings. The operator on the other end of the line went carefully through a list of pre-prepared questions as I gave my account.

A small story in the next morning's Glasgow Herald reported a number of sightings of an unexplained object in the sky to the west of the city centre that night. I can't explain what it was but at least I'm in the good company of ex-president Jimmy Carter, Muhammed Ali, The Krankies and, possibly, Jim Irwin.

The other highlights of my trips to London were visits to the Palace of Westminster. Due to Andy McMahon's limited time in the Commons, I'd never managed to visit during my tenure as editor of The Govan Press. However, after I took over the Clydebank paper I never failed to visit whenever I had a break in London.

The local MP, Hugh McCartney, much more of a political heavyweight than Andy, was one of the Labour whips in the Commons. His son, Ian, was later Minister of State for Trade in Tony Blair's government.

Hugh and I would chat over drinks in the Strangers' Bar or dine in the Harcourt Room, now renamed the Churchill Room, discussing local and national political gossip, with heavyweights of the Labour movement, such as Neil Kinnock and Arthur Scargill, popping up to chat to him every once in a while. I loved the atmosphere.

I took a special delight in the journey back to Ian's flat by taxi from the members' entrance, through the Palace of

Westminster's huge Carriage Gates, past Downing Street, up the Mall to Buckingham Palace, round the Victoria Monument, and up Constitution Hill to the Wellington Arch. It was a wonderful cab ride through British history.

While editor of *The Clydebank Press*, I was lucky enough to experience at first-hand what at the time was predicted to be a transformative moment in British politics.

As the Labour Party drifted further and further to the Left, with the election of Michael Foot as leader in 1980, four prominent members – Roy Jenkins, Shirley Williams, David Owen and Bill Rodgers, collectively known as the "Gang of Four" – split with the party. Twenty-eight Labour MPs and one Conservative eventually joined the party.

With Margaret Thatcher at the time highly unpopular and Michael Foot's eccentricity and left-wing policies making him unelectable, support for the new party began to grow throughout the country. At one point in late 1981, after forming an alliance with the Liberal Party, their popularity rating stood at more than 50 per cent.

Were the party to win the next general election, Roy Jenkins, a former Home Secretary and Chancellor of the Exchequer and most recently president of the European Commission, was the most obvious choice to become the party's prime minister. There was one problem, however, as Jenkins did not have a seat in the House of Commons.

After narrowly losing a by-election in Warrington, he set his sights on being elected to the Glasgow Hillhead seat when a by-election was forced by the death of the sitting member, Conservative Tam Galbraith. Given its national importance, the by-election was fiercely contested by all parties and, as the Hillhead constituency was geographically close to Clydebank, I was thrilled to be able to get a ticket for the election count.

The count took place at Knightswood Secondary School, where my mother had studied as a girl, and the tension was palpable. Of the eight candidates, only Labour, Conservative and Jenkins had any real chance of winning.

I managed to grab a few minutes with Jenkins before the declaration and was amazed that he was only starting to write his acceptance speech less than 15 minutes beforehand. A respected and prodigious author, he obviously felt confident in his ability to write powerful prose at speed.

When the result was announced, with the SDP winning more than a third of the vote, a beaming Jenkins was subjected to vitriolic heckling, including shouts of traitor, but he simply lit a large cigar and celebrated with his supporters.

Jenkins as Home Secretary had fundamentally changed Britain in the sixties and seventies, legalising abortion, decriminalising homosexuality, and introducing the Sex Discrimination Act and the Race Relations Act, all of which had faced strong opposition, so I'm really glad to have met him, if even for just a brief time.

Fate, however, was to rob him of the general election victory and prime minister role that the media predicted would be his that night. Tucked away on page 5 of the edition of the Glasgow *Herald* that trumpeted Jenkins' by-election success was a little story headed "Falklanders live in fear of the future" and began, "Fears of an international incident over the Argentinians who landed on South Georgia are pervading the 1800 steadfastly British Falkland islanders." Within four days, the Falklands story was front-page news and, when Britain went to war with Argentina, Margaret Thatcher's popularity soared and ended the possibility of an SDP-Liberal Alliance general election victory.

One other politician I met and chatted to at the count also made history that night, however. Early in the evening, I sat next to a smartly dressed old man and we made polite conversation until I realised he was one of the candidates. He was Lieutenant Colonel Bill Boakes, who was standing for the Public Safety Democratic Monarchist White Resident Party.

A Dunkirk veteran, Bill was an inveterate election candidate, standing for 25 parliamentary seats across 31 years. Happy to sit and chat, he came across as a kindly old grandpa rather than the mad old eccentric the media painted him to be.

That night, as we stood in the Knightswood school hall, he seemed completely unperturbed that he had made British political history when he received just five votes, a new record low for a candidate in any British parliamentary election. Even more amazing when it's considered that it meant fewer people had voted for him than had signed his nomination papers.


Around this time, my job was my life and I rarely switched off. I'd work five days a week in the office, and at weekends often spend days bent over the living room table working on new page designs or ideas for features.

I did have holidays, however, and tried where possible to switch off for a couple of weeks. A favourite destination was Ian and Janette's caravan in the South of France, a place they'd bought in the late seventies when they began to have success on the club scene.

It was on a static caravan site, nestled among the fruit trees in the countryside just inland from Argelès-sur-Mer. Now, I believe, this is a bustling seaside resort, but at the time it was a rather sleepy haven on the Mediterranean, about 20 minutes by train from the inland city of Perpignan. The area was idyllic, but it was also the scene of one of the most terrifying events of my life.

It was my second visit to the caravan. I'd travelled to France the previous year with my school friend Gordon

Blair and we'd had a lovely relaxing holiday cycling in the foothills of the Pyrenees and relaxing on the sandy beach.

In the evenings, we'd cycle down to Argelès village, where we became honorary locals in the Bar du Midi, the small town bar. Few tourists ventured into the town, preferring the more commercial beachside establishments on the coast, so the proprietor welcomed our custom. We'd cycle down to town in the twilight and return, regularly falling off our bikes along the tiny country paths in the darkness around midnight.

One local was particularly friendly. A short, stocky, ruddy-faced man with a pencil-thin moustache, his name was Damaso, and he made it very plain from the first night we met him that he wasn't French, he wasn't Spanish, he was Catalan. When we told him we were from Scotland, he immediately drew parallels between Scotland's fight for independence and the Catalans' own struggles. All three of us bonded from that moment.

The friendship was all the more strange given that Damaso was a man, probably in his 60s, who could speak no English, while we had a not-much-better command of the French language and absolutely no words of Catalan. Conversations were largely conducted by means of hand gestures and eye movements. However, it's said that the shortest distance between two people is a smile, and most of our nights in the Bar du Midi were spent laughing.

I doubt we ever saw Damaso sober, but he was one of the happiest drunks I have ever met, and we never once saw him lose his temper or become objectionable.

When Gordon and I returned to Argelès the following summer, with a colleague from Cossar Press, Stephen Patterson, we took two bottles of whisky with us, one for the bar owner and one for Damaso. Things had changed, however, as the bar had been taken over by a new proprietor, who, while not hostile, was less welcoming than the previous owner.

There was also no sign of Damaso as we entered the bar, and we wondered if the new regime had tired of hosting the town drunk. Soon after we arrived, however, his smiling florid face appeared through the doors and lit up even more when he saw us standing at the bar. We had an enjoyable evening but couldn't help feeling that the atmosphere was different.

Several nights later, we made our nightly pilgrimage to the Bar du Midi to find the mood had darkened considerably more.

In his limited English, the bar owner explained, "The English kids, they come to the town last night and they break the windows."

It seems a group of English teenagers, presumably from the seaside resort, had visited the village very late the previous night and smashed the windows of several houses and businesses.

"Nous sommes écossais," I replied in our equally painful French, desperate to distance ourselves from the troublemakers. "L'anglais," I continued, shaking my head at the idea of the Sassenach attackers.

Less than 15 minutes after we arrived, we became aware something was happening around the entrance. Throughout the summer, the concertina folding doors of the bar were fully pulled back, so the tables on the pavement became an extension of the interior. Now, on either side of the opening, groups of French youths were beginning to gather, with more turning up on their mopeds every few minutes.

They stayed outside the bar but it was plain from their steely gazes directed at our table that they believed we were responsible for the previous night's wreckage and that they planned to punish us.

I made a trip along the long narrow passage to the very

basic squat toilet at the back of the building to check if there was a possible means of escape, but found just a tiny ventilation window. Returning to my seat, I found the bar owner in a heated discussion with Gordon and Stephen.

"He says he's new to the bar and doesn't want any trouble," explained Gordon. "He wants us to leave!"

I looked across at the angry mob of youths now completely blocking the exit and began to imagine the sort of beating we were about to incur.

Then, from the corner of the bar, Damaso appeared, gesturing for us to follow him. He led us towards the door and miraculously the crowd parted. Behind them was a small black Citroen. Damaso opened the door of the car, and we bundled in, scampering across the back seat, our hot bare legs below our shorts sticking to the plastic upholstery, to find safety as quickly as possible.

The crowd stood and watched as the car pulled away, instructed I imagine by our saviour, who had called the mini cab while our heated discussion with the owner was taking place. His drunken antics may have occasionally made him a figure of fun but, for whatever reason, Damaso possessed a degree of respect in the town that saved us from, at best, a severe beating and at worst, who knows?

That night, back at the static caravan, I lay in bed and listened as mopeds buzzed about the countryside, becoming closer and then more distant, closer and then more distant, like angry mosquitos with a thirst for blood.

We never had any more trouble from the youths of Argelès. I like to imagine that night, after we left, Damaso gave them a brief history and geography lesson about "The Auld Enemy" and set them straight about the countries north and south of the Solway Firth.

Several years later, once I had moved to London and was living with my wife-to-be Chris, we returned to Argelès for a holiday in the caravan. Venturing down to the town on the first evening, we entered the Bar du Midi and I spoke to the barman, who explained there had been another change of proprietor since that unhappy night.

Where, I asked, was Damaso?

"Il est morte," he replied, sadly informing me of his death.

Without going into detail, I explained that I owed him a debt of gratitude and gave my condolences.

The next day, as we passed the bar, I had an idea. I asked the owner if he could tell me where Damaso's grave was, as I felt it would be a nice gesture to visit it and pay my respects. The bar owner was so impressed by my mark of deference that he suggested he accompany me to the graveyard and show me personally.

So it was that Chris, the bar owner and I made our way solemnly out of town, across the bridge, to the cemetery on the other side of the railway track where Damaso has been interred.

As I approached his grave, I suddenly realised I was completely unprepared for what was expected of me. Not being Catholic, I had no idea what the correct motion was to make the sign of the cross, for example. I was pretty certain it was my forehead first but was it then right, left or the stomach? Actually, was it even forehead first? I tried desperately to remember what our old Irish friend Joan Walsh used to joke. Was it "Spectacles, testicles, pocket book and watch"? Yes, it was, but is "pocket book" right or left?

As we neared the grave, I became more and more panicked that I would in some way insult Damaso and offend the bar owner with my lack of knowledge of the ritual blessing. We reached the burial plot and I stood in front of the headstone. I felt anticipation hanging in the air as I looked across at the bar owner, who smiled weakly.

Taking a deep breath, I earnestly twiddled my fingers in

the manner of Ted Rogers hosting the game show 3-2-1 and mumbled something that I believed sounded suitably sombre, ending by taking one step backwards and bowing.

The bar owner was moved to tears, and I felt proud that I'd done the moment justice. As I walked away, feeling content that I'd been able to pay respects to my rescuer, I could imagine the laughing ruddy face of Damaso enjoying my elaborate little pantomime.

# CHAPTER 8

While I loved editing a weekly local newspaper, by the age of 23 I'd had enough of living at home with my mother. I also felt it was time I moved my career on to the next stage.

Since my father's death, my mum, Betty, had become very reliant on me. She was 64 and fit and healthy, both physically and mentally, but I felt that if I didn't make the move away from Clydebank soon, it would only become more and more difficult as she grew older and more dependent on me.

She had taken to calling around my friends to check on my whereabouts if I was out late at night, which was both embarrassing to me and annoying for them, and I could only see matters getting worse as she advanced in years.

The natural next step for young West of Scotland journalists was to join the *Daily Record* or the *Glasgow Herald*, the two big Glasgow daily papers, and it had been the path taken by many of my colleagues at DC Thomson and Cossar Press. I began applying for jobs further afield, however, partly spurred by my adventures with Ian and Janette in England, and especially London, but also to put some geographical distance between Mum and me, something I felt would be beneficial if our relationship was to survive.

I applied for jobs on papers as far afield as Coventry and Plymouth and even looked to enter the expanding world of local television, answering an ad in the *UK Press Gazette* for a reporter on the Border TV early evening news show *Lookaround*.

I got as far as the interview stage with the Border job and had a phone meeting with Derek Batey, famous at the time for presenting Border's only networked ITV show, *Mr &*

*Mrs*, a lunchtime game show in which husbands and wives were quizzed to see how much they knew about their spouses' lives and loves. Derek seemed to run Border almost single-handed, and I had visions of him wearily trooping down the stairs from a flat above the studios to turn the channel off late at night.

I'm not sure if I got the interview solely because Derek was an old mate of Ian and Janette's. But rather than interrogate me about my career and aspirations, after I'd told him how much I enjoyed the nightlife of London and trips to the theatre, I recall that much of the interview was spent with him downplaying the attractions of Carlisle, the channel's base.

He was a lovely man, and I think he was attempting to steer me towards rejecting the job, rather than disappointing me by telling me my application had been unsuccessful. In the end, having tried and failed to dampen my enthusiasm, Derek suggested that local radio was a perfect apprenticeship for TV news and that I should look there as a starting point.

Perhaps it was fate, but when I successfully applied for a job it was the perfect role. Based in London, it was with my favourite childhood magazine, *TV Times*.

I have wonderful memories of my mum returning from the shops with copies of *TV Times* and *Radio Times* on a Tuesday morning. Only *TV Times* could publish ITV listings and *Radio Times* had the sole rights to print BBC schedules. So in the sixties and seventies, to get a full picture of what was on TV in the coming week, you had to buy both.

I've loved magazines and comics since a very early age. As a toddler, one of the highlights of my week was my Saturday morning trip to the shops when Dad would buy me a comic, *Jack and Jill* or *Robin*, and I'd sit quietly browsing the pages while he gossiped with a butcher pal, Johnny Russell.

I can still recall the thrill when my mum bought my first US comic book at the age of six in the Sauchiehall Street branch of Woolworths. It was the June 1966 *Detective Comics* issue featuring a cover with Batman smashing a villain in the face. Later, I became addicted to superhero titles and would use the money entrusted to me for school dinners to buy a chocolate bar and a US comic.

When I was nine, my dad gave both me and my little playmate, Fiona, sixpence (two and a half pence in decimal money) for sweets. When we got to the tiny newsagents, on the counter was the first issue of the football weekly *Shoot*, with free cardboard league ladders that allowed you to have a constant reminder of the up-to-date football tables on your wall. I talked poor Fiona into combining our sweet money and buying the magazine, which featured Bobby Moore on the cover. She had no interest in football, but sweetly handed over her sixpence, so I could indulge my love of football and magazines.

The delight I experienced each week when the two TV magazines arrived, however, topped the lot, combining as it did my two favourite things – magazines and television. Of the two, *TV Times* was my favourite. It had a more modern design, was more colourful and had better paper quality.

In 1983, I'd seen the ad for a sub-editor vacancy in the *Press Gazette* and instantly applied. As much as the idea of working on my favourite magazine excited me, I really saw it as simply a steppingstone to Fleet Street, the London district in which the majority of national newspapers were based.

I was dejected when I received a letter telling me I'd been unsuccessful but assuring me they'd keep my application on file, a promise I suspected was simply designed to lessen my disappointment.

The week of my birthday in October, however, I was thrilled to receive an invitation to London for an interview.

The meeting went well and a week later I received a job offer. I was moving to London to become a magazine journalist – albeit, I believed, for a short time until I hit national newspapers.

Mum took the news well, as I think she'd always suspected that I would leave Clydebank to develop my career, and I began a series of farewell celebrations with friends and colleagues.

When I attended my final Clydebank District Council meeting, the provost made a very gracious speech, especially given that I had been a thorn in his and his councillor's flesh for much of my tenure. He then invited me to say a few words in reply.

By this time, the Scottish Development Agency (SDA) plans to combat unemployment and revitalise the area were taking shape. It was plain that the easing of planning approval that the council had agreed would take place was threatening to have a detrimental effect on the town.

One project, in particular, proposed building a huge estate of houses in Old Kilpatrick, the prettiest and least-developed area of the burgh, and the agreement the council had struck with the SDA meant little could be done to block its construction.

Having thanked the provost for his kind words, I felt compelled to have my say about the proposals. "As you know," I began, "my father served this town with great distinction, as a councillor and eventually as burgh treasurer, for many years. He would have been appalled, as I am, at the dereliction of duty that the majority of you are guilty of."

The smile on the face of the provost and his inner circle turned to a look of rage as I continued, "To have handed dominion to an unelected authority, leaving the people of Clydebank powerless to stop this sprawling development, is disgraceful." As I continued my tirade, I almost felt like I was channelling my father, and it felt great.

As we left the chamber, many of the councillors shook their heads at this kid who had so rudely insulted their hospitality, but one or two whispered words of encouragement. I'd well and truly burned my bridges, but I had no regrets as I headed for a new life in London.

I arrived in the capital on Sunday 16 January 1983 and booked into a hotel in Paddington. The next morning was a historic one for me as I prepared for my first day at *TV Times* and, coincidentally, for British television.

I switched off the alarm clock in the tiny top-floor room of the hotel, an establishment I discovered as the week went on that I was sharing with a number of the area's prostitutes, crossed the squeaky floorboards to the TV and turned on BBC1 to watch the first edition of *BBC Breakfast Time*, the UK's first regular breakfast TV show.

It was a time of massive change in British television. Just a few months earlier, Channel 4 had gone on air, offering 25 per cent more TV channels than had ever existed before, and two weeks later TV-am, the ITV breakfast channel, would make its debut. As TV was expanding, it felt like the right time to be starting my new job.

I'd been sent scant details about my working week by my new employers, but I had no worries – I was just thrilled to be in London working at *TV Times*. I'd been given a start time of 10.00 am, presumably as this was my first day, but allowed too much time for travelling and appeared at the offices in Tottenham Court Road more than half an hour earlier than arranged.

Taking the lift to the third floor, I discovered that I was almost alone in the huge open-plan office.

"Take a seat," I was instructed by one of the boys in the post room, "most of the team won't be in until ten."

A 10 o'clock start on a Monday – very civilised, I thought – and as the hour approached, the office began to fill up. I was shown around and introduced to my new colleagues. At lunchtime, we headed for the local pub, The Bedford Arms, where I had a chance to have a more relaxed conversation with the other writers and sub-editors.

Realising how little I knew about my new working conditions, while sinking a pint of lager I asked what the office hours were.

"Well, today is ten until six," said Geoffrey, a slightly camp middle-aged man with an accent that wouldn't have been out of place broadcasting on BBC radio in the fifties. "Tomorrow is ten until seven-thirty."

That made more sense, I thought. I couldn't see any way that I'd be earning the excellent salary I was if the hours were 10 til six every day.

"Wednesday is back to a ten o'clock start and a six o'clock finish," Geoffrey continued, "and Thursday is ten until half past four."

My eyebrows rose at another pleasant surprise. "And Friday?" I asked.

"Oh, we don't work on a Friday, my dear boy," replied Geoffrey with a laugh.

I looked around the high poseur bar table that we were all standing around. Everyone was nodding. Was this one of those practical jokes you play on new recruits, I thought, like sending an apprentice for a replacement bubble for the spirit level. I broke away from our group and asked a couple of random members of staff I'd been introduced to earlier what the Friday working hours were and they confirmed Geoffrey's story.

I was gobsmacked. Not only was I being paid much more than I had been in Clydebank, where I'd often worked seven days a week, I was only working four days at *TV Times* and finishing at 4.30 on Thursday.

I later learned that the reason for the amazingly good contract terms was the power of the unions in the seventies.

The duopoly that *TV Times* and *Radio Times* had, as far as printing TV schedules was concerned, meant the two magazines had circulations that rivalled those of national newspapers. This had led to the union members at the two titles winning the same kind of working conditions as the giant Fleet Street papers, resulting in high wages and low hours. I thought I'd died and gone to heaven.

The four-day week had attracted many talented writers to join *TV Times* as sub-editors, as it allowed them three days a week to indulge their favourite passions, while still being paid an impressive remuneration. So it was that the team included a number of playwrights and authors, who from Monday to Thursday would edit the listings pages of a regional edition of the magazine before turning to more serious projects over the long weekend.

Missing the smell of newspaper ink and the roar of the printing press, I spent the weekends of my first few months working as a freelancer in Fleet Street, where I was planning eventually to continue my paper career. On Friday, I worked at *The Sun*, and on Saturdays, it was *The News of the World*, both located just off Fleet Street in Bouverie Street.

At the time, *The News of the World* was edited by Derek Jameson, who had successfully increased circulation on the *Daily Express* before launching the more downmarket *Daily Star*. A few years later, Jameson went on to have a career as a TV and radio star.

One Saturday, I was working on the sports desk when a bundle of early editions of *The News of the Screws*, as it was affectionately known, came up from the press room. One by one, as journalists picked a copy off the top of the pile, they began to laugh. As more and more of the newsroom ventured across to collect a copy, what had begun as a few stifled snorts, swelled to a wave of chuckles and finally exploded into a roar, until the whole office was awash with helpless laughter.

I picked a copy of the paper off the unwrapped parcel and read the headline, "UFOs lands in Suffolk", with the subhead, "And that's official". It was obvious from the reaction, in the same way a football manager can lose the dressing room, Jameson had lost the newsroom, who felt under his editorship the paper was becoming a joke. He was sacked by Rupert Murdoch a few months later.

Ironically, nearly 40 years on, the story, involving the sighting by members of the United States Air Force of a landed UFO in Rendlesham Forest, has become famous worldwide, powered by the internet, and is known as Britain's Roswell.

The four-day week wasn't the only perk of the job at *TV Times*. We also enjoyed a two-hour lunch stretching from 12.30 until 2.30, allowing for a great deal of alcohol to be consumed. Senior magazine editors would often take even longer breaks and return from the pub or restaurant much the worse for wear.

One deputy editor was so famous for returning aggressive and expletive-filled page proofs to subs after lunch that every effort was made to ensure that he received his quota of pages before midday.

Drinking wasn't restricted to an out-of-office activity either. Some mornings, and most afternoons, the senior team would disappear into one of the many executive offices that lined the right-hand side of the open-plan area for a booze-fuelled meeting.

At the end of my first week, I was astonished to see a packed trolley delivering champagne, gin, cigarettes and cigars to each of the executive offices. How we ever managed to get a magazine out I'll never know, but that was journalism in the eighties.

After a couple of weeks living at the Paddington hotel, I moved into Ian and Janette's one-bedroom flat in Oxford and Cambridge Mansions, on the other side of Edgware

Road. I was comfortable in the building, having stayed there many times when visiting London. I also knew the couple who owned the flat above: John Hobbs, who directed such BBC comedy hits as *Butterflies*, *Bread* and *'Allo 'Allo*, and his partner Iain McCorquodale, who was the Deputy Crown Jeweller.

I began hunting for a flat of my own to buy almost immediately, using the underground to quickly move from one area of central London to another, heading below ground in one district and popping up a few minutes later in another, with little idea of the relative distance between the various properties.

After seeing half a dozen potential flats, I eventually found just what I had been looking for. Leaving Ian and Janette's red brick Victorian mansion block one morning, I'd made the short journey to the Bakerloo Line station in Edgware Road before heading down in the lift to the northern platform and boarding the train to Marylebone station. From there, I walked up Lisson Grove, famous as the birthplace of Eliza Doolittle in George Bernard Shaw's *Pygmalion*, towards St John's Wood. Turning right into Rossmore Road, I met the estate agent and was shown into the ground-floor flat in a four-storey brick "period building".

The price was just about manageable, thanks to the £1,000 I could pay as a deposit, courtesy of a scratch card win I'd had while editor of *The Clydebank Press*.

I was seriously thinking of making a bid, and left the estate agent at the front door to check out the surrounding area and the local amenities. I walked back down Lisson Grove, but instead of heading left at the bottom to return to Marylebone Station I carried on to the foot of the Grove. After just a few minutes I reached Marylebone Road with its constant stream of busy traffic.

What could I see? I thought.

Looking left, in the distance was Baker Street and Madam Tussauds; to my right was the Westway rising above Paddington, and straight across, to my astonishment, was the end of the Old Marylebone Road mansion block I was currently living in.

Far from the lengthy journey by foot and Tube, the new flat was in fact only a five-minute walk away. I made a bid that day and secured my new home.


My career at *TV Times* was a world away from the pressures of editing a local newspaper. But I enjoyed it and was soon put in charge of the listings pages of one of the regional editions, Tyne Tees, the ITV region that at that time served the North East of England.

Each of the numerous ITV franchises had its own sub-editor, who oversaw the listings pages for that regional edition. It involved receiving the time-and-title TV programme schedules and combining them with a short précis of often pages of information provided by the TV companies about individual programmes. All the work was done on typewriters and then the typed pages were sent down to the printers by motorbike courier, before returning as printed pages to be edited by pen, incorporating changes made to the ITV company's schedules. The final "clean" pages were then biked back to the printers for the alterations to be incorporated and the details published.

I was proud of my pages, and edited every small piece of programme information as if it was a major article. Others were not so fastidious. Mitch, who oversaw the Grampian edition, serving the North of Scotland, had pages that contained a number of Gaelic programmes, which had series billings written in the Celtic language. He would copy as many words as were required to fill the space, with no idea what they meant or whether they made sense, ending with an ellipsis, three little dots. To my knowledge, he never received any complaints.

Eager to advance my career, I applied for promotions within the magazine and found myself suffering from a reverse form of sex discrimination when, despite being informed I was perfect for the role, I was told I'd failed to win a role because it was felt there were not enough women in executive positions.

I was happy, however, at *TV Times*, and outside of work I was enjoying life too. Far from being lonely, as I'd feared I might be in London, when not busy working at the magazine and my shifts at *The Sun* and *The News of the World*, I was happy exploring my adopted city.

I'd also become a regular at the pub that Ian and Janette had introduced me to near their flat, The Beehive in Homer Street. A tiny room about the size of a large sitting room, the pub was frequented by an incredibly diverse clientele, ranging from dustbin men and postmen to lawyers and city traders. It became a regular haunt for the 10 years I lived in central London.

During my first summer in the city, Ian and Janette rented their flat out to a stage manager, John Gregory, and his dancer girlfriend, but soon after they shook on the deal the pair broke up, leaving John alone in the flat. Unhappy at the thought of a footloose-and-fancy-free twenty-something living in their home, Ian asked me to keep an eye on John, which resulted in the pair of us becoming firm friends and drinking buddies in The Beehive, often enjoying lock-ins (after-hours drinking, for the uninitiated) until the early hours of the morning.

It was a relationship that was to last, as I was best man at John's marriage to his wife, Jan, and godfather to his two boys, James and Jack.

John was a hugely talented stage manager who started his career in the theatre but branched out into television. It was a combination of talents that later led to him regularly stage managing the televised *Royal Variety Performance* and, following his death, tribute being paid to him at the annual BAFTA TV Awards ceremony.

At the time we met, John was stage manager at London Weekend Television (LWT), which held the Saturday and Sunday franchise for the capital and produced programmes for the whole ITV network, working on a comedy panel game called *Punchlines*, with the comedian Lennie Bennett.

I'd attend every recording, two a night, then nip up to the LWT bar to enjoy drinks with John and the team, before sharing John's executive cab back to Marylebone. At the same time, Ian and Janette were recording *The Krankies Klub*, a Saturday teatime show, also filmed at ITV, so I was often out a couple of nights a week at LWT.

In addition to my shifts at *The Sun* and *The News of the World*, just before John's appearance, I'd taken on another freelance job. One of the senior editors at *TV Times*, Jim Bush, had a contract with *The Sun*, then the UK's largest selling daily newspaper, to supply each day's listings. Jim would subcontract younger members of the magazine to write the content, taking a percentage for himself.

Jim had approached me to write the Tuesday TV page and I'd gratefully agreed. All went well until my nightly visits to The Beehive and the TV studios began to become a regular arrangement. As the weeks went by, however, the time allotted to *The Sun* work reduced dramatically and, I'm ashamed to say, so did the quality of the prose.

Most of the information about the schedules was available via my *TV Times* contacts and, as the magazine had gone to press before work had to be completed on the newspaper page, it was pretty straightforward. The one exception was a "The Sun says" review comment that had to be added to every film.

My normal destination for that insight was a well-thumbed edition of *Halliwell's Film Guide*, the book that was the number one source of film reviews in those pre-internet years. On the very odd occasion when *Halliwell's* couldn't provide me with an option, I would take an educated guess, evaluating all the known facts.

One night, however, under pressure of a beckoning pint with John, I got it badly wrong. I had all but finished *The Sun*'s Tuesday TV page and just had to add the short review of an Australian film called *Masquerade* showing late at night on some ITV regions. The problem was, I couldn't find it in *Halliwell's*.

OK, I thought, it's late night, it's only showing in a small number of regions and it's Australian, not known at the time as a producer of quality films. So I wrote, "The Sun says: Time for a cup of cocoa and an early night!" Job done, it was off to The Beehive.

That weekend, however, I visited Great Yarmouth, where The Krankies were topping the bill at the Britannia Pier. As I entered the house they were renting, Ian and comedian Al Dean were watching TV.

"Great to see you," shouted Ian over his shoulder from the settee. "Grab a seat. We're just watching a great movie I recorded the other night; it's Australian, called *Harlequin*."

"It's strange," said Al, "*The Sun* said it was a load of crap."

As my face began to turn red, betraying my involvement, Ian twisted round to face me. "Don't you write *The Sun* TV page?" he asked accusingly.

I was forced to admit my guilt.

A week later, another rushed TV page resulted in me attributing the Kingsley Amis book on which the film *Lucky Jim* was based to that other renowned British author Graham Greene.

"*The Sun* has had complaints from everyone from Kingsley Amis's agent to Graham Greene himself," Jim Bush claimed, when he confronted me with the error.

Whether it was true or not, and I find it hard to believe Graham Greene used *The Sun* to guide his TV viewing, my time was up and I handed the Tuesday TV page over to another, more dedicated, writer.

My evenings with John may have put an end to my freelance work but that was a small cost to pay for a friendship that was to last until John's death.

When Ian and Janette returned to London from summer season, John was forced to find somewhere to live and I offered him the bed settee in the living room "for a week or two". The fortnight extended to a month, then two, then three, and in the end I had a lodger for nearly a year. It was great fun, however, and I wouldn't have changed it for the world.

Tragically, John died on the evening of his birthday in 2003. Having gone out for a couple of drinks with friends from the London Studios where he was working, he returned home and dropped dead in his office aged just 48. James and Jack were just 13 and 11.

I was honoured to be asked by his colleagues to be part of the team that arranged John's memorial service, which was to take place at the actor's church, St Paul's in Covent Garden, the setting for the opening scene of George Bernard Shaw's *Pygmalion* and its equally famous musical adaptation *My Fair Lady*.

The organising committee had met on one of the upper floors of the London Studios building that overlooked the Thames in Waterloo a number of months before to discuss the event and how it should be structured. As you would expect from a bunch of TV executives, the meeting came up with hugely exciting and innovative ideas for the service but it was an idea towards the end of the discussion that took my breath away.

"Why don't we end the memorial service by firing a glitter bomb," proposed one of the group around the table.

I immediately had my doubts about the viability and propriety of detonating such a device that would cascade glitter throughout the seventeenth-century Inigo Jones-designed building, but before I could raise my worries the room erupted in agreement that this would be the perfect finale. It would have felt churlish to have disagreed.

The event itself was a beautiful tribute to John's life and work. Hosted by Jeremy Beadle, who John worked with on his TV prank series *Beadle's About*, the church was filled with TVs showing video tributes to John from the likes of *Who Wants to Be a Millionaire's* Chris Tarrant and *So You Think You Can Dance* creator and panellist Nigel Lythgoe, who John had worked with as a dancer before teaming up again when John stage-managed Royal Variety Shows that Nigel produced and directed.

There were clips from shows that John had worked on, plus live music from the cast of the Queen musical *We Will Rock You*, a favourite of John's, and a less-spectacular eulogy from yours truly, in which I recounted our early days together in London.

The memorial did indeed end with a glitter bomb that blanketed the entire church in a sparkling blizzard. Far from being peeved by the performance, the vicar concluded that he would have to consider whether to introduce it to his regular Sunday services. I'm so glad I didn't express my initial unease at the suggestion. The day was an unforgettable event and John would have loved the glitzy final flourish.

A few months after John first moved into my flat in Rossmore Road, I met my wife-to-be, Chris, and eventually she moved into the flat too.

I'd been visiting Ian and Janette who were summer seasoning in Great Yarmouth when I was introduced to an Australian girl, Nerida, who was touring Europe and had dropped into Yarmouth to look up an old boyfriend who was playing in the theatre band.

We'd got on well and she took me up on an offer to stay at my flat when she came back to London. Eventually Nerida got a job at a local hospital, The Nightingale off Lisson Grove, and moved into staff accommodation. Chris was a nurse at the same hospital. Nerida introduced us and we hit it off immediately.

I'd had several girlfriends over the years, with varying degrees of success. I was so pleased that my very first date at high school agreed to go out with me, for example, that I took her to the cinema without checking on the content of the film that was showing, *The Triple Echo*. As I sidled closer and closer to her, slowly rearranging my arm so that my hand was creeping over her shoulder, any developing passion was immediately extinguished as on-screen Oliver Reed attempted to rape a cross-dressing army deserter. Not the perfect first date, and not surprisingly it was our last.

A few years and several girlfriends later, I'd been admiring a girl who boarded my morning train to work every day halfway between Clydebank and Glasgow. I couldn't believe my luck when I saw her in a pub while out with friends in nearby Bearsden.

Emboldened by more pints of Dutch Courage than you'd find in an Amsterdam canal, I approached her and asked for her phone number. To my amazement, she wrote her details on my business card and passed it back to me.

When I called the number the next day, I found I was through to the switchboard at the main Glasgow branch of the Bank of Scotland. However, knowing my dream girl had the uncommon name Ailish, I managed to embarrassingly explain my quest and worked my way through various phone connections, all eager to help young love flourish, until I finally got to the subject of my fascination, who agreed to a date.

We met under the clock at Glasgow's Buchanan Bus

Station and I led her to Epicure, at the time one of Glasgow's top steak restaurants and an establishment I felt sure would impress. It didn't. It transpired that Ailish was something I'd never come across in the west of Scotland in the seventies – a vegetarian. Another romance ended on the first date!

I had more luck a couple of years later with another girl I'd met in a bar. Her name was Trina and she was working as a waitress in a cocktail bar, much like the heroine in the Human League song of the time, and had overheard me explaining to friends that Ian and Janette had a new catchphrase they planned to introduce viewers to when they joined the BBC children's series *Crackerjack* the following week.

"What was that word?" she asked.

"Fandabidozi," I repeated, gazing back at her pretty face. "And if you can remember it by the end of the evening, you'll win a star prize," I promised.

Come the end of the night, she returned to our table and repeated a word that vaguely resembled Fandabidozi. It was enough encouragement for me.

"Fantastic," I told her. "You've won a night out with me." It was the cheesiest chat-up line I'd ever used but it resulted in a string of dates.

Funnily enough, The Krankies' catchphrase, Fandabidozi, was the brainchild of one of Ian and Janette's dancers, Karen Long, another girl with whom I had a relationship in my teenage years, when she and I hooked up during an eventful holiday in Jersey.

She had been travelling in a car to a gig at Jollees, the Stoke-on-Trent nightclub, with Ian and Janette during a Krankies tour, when the idea of a catchphrase for Janette's character Jimmy had arisen. Janette admitted that the BBC had suggested they needed one but that after weeks and weeks of head scratching they'd still failed to produce a word or phrase they felt worked.

Karen thought for a few seconds and then confidently announced, "Fandabidozi."

It was a gibberish word that just popped into her head. But everyone in the car agreed that it sounded good, so Janette, as Jimmy, started using it when the series began. Within days, children were shouting it at the pair in the street and fan letters were arriving, signing off "Fandabidozi".

The word has now slipped into common usage and Karen's creation has even been added to the Collins Dictionary, with the definition: "*informal* An expression of admiration or enthusiasm. Popularised by The Krankies, a Scottish comedy duo."

Despite the stream of girlfriends and flings over the previous six or seven years, before I met Chris I'd only really had one long-term relationship, Hazel, who I'd begun dating in the final year at high school but had broken up with many years before I left for London.

Chris and I were comfortable in each other's company from the very first time we met, and love grew over the coming weeks as we spent more and more time together. Very soon, Chris was spending an increasing number of nights at Rossmore Road.

Together we'd spend our evenings in The Beehive, often with John Gregory joining us, with an eclectic bunch of fellow revellers. There was Roger, an art restorer who worked with Old Masters, and his wife Nita; Robin, who became my lawyer, and his wife Chrissie, who was British skeet shooting champion many years running; and Stuart, a bank manager turned horticulturist, and his wife Joy, a medical secretary.

They were joined by other characters such as Albie, a postman, Dave and Sid, who were former binmen, and by the last of a dying generation of Oxford Street barrow merchants, including Harry the Fruit and his father-in-law, the eyepatch-wearing Harry the Fish, elder statesman of the stalls. After months of frequenting the pub, I only felt truly welcome when one night Harry the Fish nodded acknowledgement as I entered.

In addition, there was American Ron, who was head of human resources for the US Navy in Europe, and the very elderly Richard, a former Chef de Mission (team manager) for the British Olympic team, who always believed the likeable Ron's job was a cover for CIA operations.

I'm sure I've left some regulars out, but I think the list gives some idea of the amazing mix of people who used the tiny Marylebone pub.

Chris was suddenly beginning to spend the bulk of her time at my small one-bedroom flat, still shared with John, and a revolving cast of other friends and acquaintances, who would sleep a night now and then on a camp bed in the tiny kitchen.

When it got to the point that Chris was simply visiting her nurses' flat to pick up the mail, we decided that we needed to buy a larger flat together and I began to look around the area in search of "For Sale" signs.

Having spent a great deal of time at Ian and Janette's home in Oxford and Cambridge Mansions, it seemed an obvious starting point to look at those buildings and the other mansion blocks just east of the Edgware Road Bakerloo station. Being on the more sought-after south side of Marylebone Road, the estate agents advertised these one- and two-bedroomed dwellings as "apartments" rather than flats.

I set out with a notebook, prepared to write the contact details for estate agents with apartments for sale and almost immediately bumped into Iain McCorquodale, who lived with his partner John Hobbs in the one-bedroom flat above Ian and Janette.

Jotting down numbers, I explained to Ian what I was doing.

"John and I are looking to move to a house in Wembley and we're looking for a buyer for our flat," he explained.

It was perfect timing. We sorted the sale out without having the fuss or the cost of involving an estate agent and in a few months we were moving into the flat directly above Ian and Janette.

We loved our new one-bedroom flat, and were thrilled to have a balcony, albeit overlooking busy Old Marylebone Road. Entering the block, with its plush red carpet and polished wooden bannisters, our flat was up one flight on the first floor. The flat's front door off the landing led to a long windowless corridor that ran the full length of the apartment. Directly on the left as you entered was the living room and off that, the small dining room, just large enough to accommodate a table and eight, at a push, chairs. Turning in the other direction at the front door took you first to the bedroom on the left, then to a small toilet, followed by a bathroom and at the bottom of the corridor the kitchen, with a window looking out at a back wall of the block.

Our close proximity to Ian and Janette, who were directly below us, meant we were in and out of each other's flats on a daily basis. If Ian was low on tomato puree for a Bolognese, he'd nip up to borrow ours, while if we found we had a missing ingredient in a curry recipe, Ian would lend it to his upstairs neighbours from his extensive spice collection.

We also had some other rather-more-exotic residents in the block. When we first moved in, we were aware that the red light in the window of the flat above was probably more than a design feature, but the thick Victorian ceilings meant we were never disturbed by any of the carnal commerce taking place overhead.

The flat was relatively near Paddington station, and Old Marylebone Road led on to Sussex Gardens, which had a reputation for hotels where working girls would offer their services. The ladies who based themselves in Oxford and Cambridge Mansions were, however, much more discreet and upmarket.

Soon after we moved in, the flat opposite Ian and Janette on the ground floor was sold and the owner rented it out. It became obvious from the flow of gentlemen visitors that the new occupant was also a member of the world's oldest profession but more worryingly they also appeared to be involved in some other dubious dealings.

Men would appear on the steps of the block, furtively buzz the intercom and the flat's resident would discreetly cross the hall to answer the door. She'd hand the caller a small package and they would skulk silently back down the steps and head off at speed away from the building.

As the weeks went by and the clandestine visits increased, we began to suspect that the block was being used as part of a drugs operation and we started to consider contacting the police.

One day, Chris was returning from work and as she readied her key to unlock the main entrance door, she saw a small Asian man buzzing the intercom at the top of the steps and the door being answered by the ground-floor tenant.

"Come in, Doctor," the woman, clad in a fluffy dressing gown, said welcomingly. "Thank you for coming."

As Chris passed the man in the hall, she looked across at him and he cowered, as if to shield his face from her gaze.

"Well, that's a turn up," said Chris, as I met her at the door of our flat. "Either the little man who owns the gift shop on Edgware Road is a closet physician, or he's paying for sex in the ground floor flat!"

A few months later, the owner of the flat appeared at our

door in a state of hysteria. She asked Chris to follow her downstairs to look at the apartment. Showing her into the back bedroom, she threw open the door to reveal a built-in wardrobe with the doors removed, the inside painted black, and chains and handcuffs attached to the wall.

The police were called but there was little they could do as the tenant had done a runner. They did, however, solve the mystery of the shady front door visitors that we believed were drug dealers. They were, the police explained, recruited by the madam to populate local BT phone boxes with business cards advertising the various services available from the girls she employed. The small packages being exchanged were bundles of the cards destined for the walls of the red call boxes.

As well as sharing some comical moments involving our call-girl neighbours, our close proximity to Ian and Janette meant we spent many evenings in The Beehive with them, followed by either a lock-in or late-night cheese and biscuits, either in their flat or ours.

Once a fortnight, if they were in town, we'd accompany Janette to meet Ian after his Water Rats meeting, which gave us the opportunity of meeting some true showbiz legends.

The Grand Order of the Water Rats is a British entertainment industry charitable organisation formed back in the late nineteenth century by two music hall comedians. Coincidentally, it held its first meetings at The Magpie pub in Sunbury-on-Thames, just over an hour's walk from the town where Chris and I made our home after leaving London.

Over the years, most major British entertainers, and many top international stars, have been members, including Charlie Chaplin, Bob Hope and Laurel and Hardy. When Ian joined the organisation in the early eighties, TV celebrities such as Jimmy Tarbuck, Max Bygraves, boxer

Henry Cooper, Danny La Rue, Les Dawson, *Are You Being Served* star John Inman, Ken Dodd, *Dad's Army* creator Jimmy Perry and Tommy Cooper were all members.

After the meetings ended, we would sit with Ian and Janette and listen to fascinating tales about amazing careers in show business.

One evening we found ourselves sitting with comedian and actor Roy Hudd, a huge star of TV and radio from the sixties to the eighties and later best known for playing undertaker Archie Shuttleworth in *Coronation Street.*

When still a young schoolboy, I'd listened under the bed covers to a late-night radio programme in which Roy had told host John Dunn about an astonishing event in his life. His story had stayed with me all those years and that night I couldn't resist asking him to recall it for our group.

"For years I'd had a recurring dream," Roy explained to us. "It wasn't unpleasant in any way; it just involved me walking about a house and staring out into an illuminated garden, before heading to the basement where I was being stared at by numerous images of myself."

"A number of years ago," he continued, "friends of mine moved into a new house in Brixton and invited my wife and me to visit them, telling me they thought it would be interesting for me to see. Intrigued, Ann and I drove to the address and, as we arrived, I was stunned by what I saw. It was the house from my dreams.

"When our friend met me at the door, I said to him, 'I know this house. I dream about it' and I went on to describe the layout of the house perfectly, without entering any of the rooms."

There was another shock to come, however, as Roy explained to our enthralled group why his friend had been so keen on him seeing the house. "It turned out that it had been owned by Dan Leno, possibly the most famous music hall comedian of his day."

Roy added that as well as being a comedian Leno had also been a clog dancer, and he assumed that he probably rehearsed in front of mirrors in the basement, which would explain the multiple images in his dream. Later he also learnt that Leno was one of the first people in London to string up external electrical lighting when he held outdoor parties, which explained the "illuminated garden".

Roy, who went on to write a number of books and articles about the music hall giant, who himself was a member of the Water Rats, was convinced that he was the reincarnation of Dan Leno, and after hearing his story, not one of us was in the position to disagree!

The highlight of the Water Rats' years was the Grand Ball, held in the Great Room at London's prestigious Grosvenor House Hotel. It was a boozy affair that started early in the evening and ran through to the early hours of the following morning, when kippers were served for breakfast. Chris and I attended in the mid-eighties when one of the honoured guests was Christiaan Barnard, internationally famous for having performed the world's first heart transplant, an event I remember delighting the world in 1967 when I was just eight.

With her background as a theatre nurse, Chris was keen to meet the legendary cardiac surgeon and nudged her way through the celebrities towards his table. After waiting while a queue of well-wishers chatted to him, she eventually reached the great man himself.

Chris offered her hand to shake his but, before she could say a word, he asked, "And do you have a heart condition too?"

It seemed his entire evening had been spent answering medical queries from ageing Rats and their guests. At the time, Chris was irritated by the question but, on reflection, it was obvious that addressing a 20-something woman, around the same age as his stunning dinner companion, he was simply having a laugh.

As well as our Sunday evening visits to the Water Rats, Chris and I would often attend recordings of shows The Krankies were involved in. One favourite was the BBC game show *Blankety Blank*, hosted at the time by the wonderful Les Dawson, a lovely man whose sparkling conversation we also enjoyed after Water Rats meetings.

Ian and Janette had appeared on the show several times, both with its first host Terry Wogan and with Les, including a memorable evening when Kenny Everett rudely insulted Janette, resulting in a furious Ian following him into the toilet and slamming him against the wall. As a young man, Ian had a very quick temper, which calmed down as he grew older, but insulting Janette is something no one will ever get away with.

One memorable recording of *Blankety Blank* saw The Krankies join Christopher Biggins, later famous as an *I'm a Celebrity* King of the Jungle, and Barbara Windsor, at the time best known for her many appearances in the *Carry On* comedy film series, before her career was transformed playing Peggy Mitchell in the soap *EastEnders*.

Chris and I had first met Biggins when Ian and Janette appeared in pantomime with him at the Alhambra Theatre in Bradford. After the shows, the entire cast would migrate to an isolated pub on the edge of a moor.

Amazingly, the camp iridescent realm of pantomime sat cheek by jowl with the butch cloth cap world of the Yorkshire working man for nightly lock-ins that stretched into the wee small hours.

On meeting Chris for the first time, and discovering she was a nurse, Biggins immediately dropped his trousers in the middle of the pub, surrounded by beer-drinking workmen, to reveal his varicose veins and beg her opinion. It was an incongruous but hilarious moment.

When we met him again at *Blankety Blank*, he was

delighted to see us and suggested Ian and Janette, Barbara Windsor, Chris and I should all join him and his partner Neil for a dinner party at their house in Hackney.

At the time, I assumed that we were only being mentioned out of politeness and that should the dinner party take place the invitation wouldn't be extended to Chris and me, but Biggins was as good as his word and the following week Ian nipped upstairs to our flat to tell us he'd been in touch to arrange the details.

The night of the dinner party, Chris was working a late shift at the hospital, so Ian, Janette and I arranged to pick up Barbara in a taxi at her mews house near Marylebone High Street, just a few minutes from our own flats.

On the way to Hackney, I explained to Barbara that I was best man at my pal Ronnie's wedding the following day and that I had to make sure I didn't overindulge with the wine.

"Don't worry," Barbara chuckled and assured me, "I'll be your motherly influence for the evening."

Remembering the ongoing discussion about Biggins' varicose veins, when she arrived at the dinner party sometime after the rest of us, Chris thought it would be funny to appear at the door, masked up, empty syringe in hand, claiming she was there to inject his enlarged veins.

She was shocked, however, when, led upstairs to Biggins' mezzanine dining room overlooking his large colourful lounge, fully dressed in her medical garb with syringe in hand, she found that she was attending a meal not simply with Biggins, his partner Neil, Barbara, Ian and Janette and me, but with several other famous faces she had never met before.

Jacqueline Pearce, who a decade earlier had played the evil but sexy Servalan in the BBC sci-fi series *Blake's 7*, was one of those sitting around the table. Now in her mid-40s, but still with her striking looks and distinctive cropped hair, she was accompanied by a young man who had seen many fewer summers than she had.

Also joining us, with his wife Moya, was George Layton, at the time writing the sitcoms *Don't Wait Up*, for Nigel Havers and Tony Britton, and *Executive Stress*, for Penelope Keith and Geoffrey Palmer, but probably best known as medical student Paul Collier in the sixties ITV comedy series *Doctor in the House*.

The final guest was an extremely camp Church of England bishop, who shall remain nameless.

Throughout the evening, as I stretched for my wine glass, Barbara would reach out and lay her hand on mine, reminding me that I had an important engagement the following day. It was a thoroughly enjoyable evening, as you would expect with Chris Biggins as the host, but I'll never forget the peculiar experience of having a *Carry On* films legend smack my hand as she acted as my surrogate mother for the night.

Funnily enough, some months later, Barbara bumped into Chris in the street near the King Edward VII Hospital where Chris was working and asked her how my best man's speech had gone. It was typical of the caring, friendly woman she was.

More than 25 years later, when I was editor-in-chief of *TV Times*, I had the pleasure of hosting a box each year at the annual *Carols with the Stars* charity concert at the Royal Albert Hall, and Barbara and her husband Scott accepted an invitation to the event.

In the intervening years, Barbara had found new fame as *EastEnders'* Peggy Mitchell, and I requested to have the couple in my box for the concert. After we were all seated, I mentioned to Barbara that we'd met before and that we'd attended a dinner party at Biggins' house.

She smiled and nodded in recognition, but it appeared to be more out of politeness than genuine recollection. Scott appeared very protective of her that evening and on a number of occasions she seemed to not be fully engaged with the conversation, while always being pleasant and courteous.

It was less than six months later that we learnt with the rest of Britain that she was suffering from Alzheimer's disease and sadly three years to the week after our carol concert meeting, she died at the age of 83.

While she has a place in the nation's hearts as the ditzy blonde whose bikini top pinged off while exercising in *Carry on Camping* and the East End matriarch who screamed, "Get outta my pub," in the Queen Vic, to me she'll always be my substitute mother.

Coincidentally, we also regularly bumped into another *EastEnders* legend in the late eighties and early nineties. Wendy Richard, who had played Pauline Fowler in the series since the very beginning, and before that had found fame as the junior ladies-wear assistant Miss Brahms in the hit BBC department store comedy *Are You Being Served?*, was a semi-regular in The Beehive, where she could often be found playing cribbage at a weekend.

We weren't great buddies, but she knew Chris and I to nod to and we'd exchange the odd word. We knew her *Are You Being Served?* co-star John Inman, who played the show's camp Mr Humphries, a little better, as he was a member of the Water Rats with Ian and he'd been round to Oxford and Cambridge Mansions for drinks.

In 1993, when we sold our flat, after our son Alexander was born, a friend from The Beehive offered us an apartment he owned in a block nearby to use until we could move to the house in Surrey that we were buying. Only after we moved in did we learn that the rental fee we were being charged for the accommodation, although probably a fair rate for the area, was far from "mates' rates".

When we met up with Ian and Janette, shortly after we'd

moved in, they mentioned that they'd hosted John and Wendy one afternoon on their boat and that the conversation had turned to the amount of rent we were being charged for the temporary apartment.

"John and Wendy were both shocked at the amount you were being asked to pay for that flat," confided Ian.

I thought about the conversation for a second and then smiled. "If you had told me as a 12-year-old back in 1972, that one day Miss Brahms and Mr Humphreys from *Are You Being Served?* would be discussing the rental fee I was paying for a flat in London," I laughed, "I would never have believed you."

# CHAPTER 9

While Chris and I were enjoying living in Oxford and Cambridge Mansions and spending our evenings and weekends with Ian and Janette, I was also turning my shorter work hours and longer weekends to my advantage.

While others spent them in the pub, the long lunchtimes I enjoyed were allowing me to develop a number of creative activities. For example, Cliff Parker, a lovely pipe-smoking colleague from Yorkshire, who, through an agent, wrote comedy books and was involved in a huge number of innovative projects, passed me an opportunity he had been offered but at the time was too busy to accept.

It involved writing Halloween-related jokes for Cadbury's small foil-wrapped chocolate bars. It was right up my street, and earned me a nice bit of pocket money for supplying such hackneyed cringe-worthy gags as "What's a ghost's favourite dessert? Answer: I scream".

Another project I embarked on at that time was to write a book of TV trivia questions. Quiz games and books were all the rage, fuelled by the recent success of the *Trivial Pursuit* board game.

*TV Times* had a massive library of cuttings, from national newspapers and magazines, which was used by writers and sub-editors to research and check facts about programmes and celebrities for articles. Having access to this huge repository of TV information and the old issues of *TV Times*, which stretched back to the 1950s, I was in the perfect position to research a quiz book.

Every lunchtime, as my colleagues evacuated the building for their two-hour-plus lunches, I would gulp down my sandwich and head to the office library to begin my daily harvest of trivia questions.

I had compiled several hundred when I was called in to a meeting with the assistant editor, Eddie Pedder, whose secretary told me simply that he wanted to see me to discuss my quiz questions. I'd kept news of what I was up to at lunchtime in the library to a small group of friends, but it was obvious word had got out and the game was up.

"I gather you're writing a TV trivia book," he said, getting straight to the point.

"That's right," I answered guiltily, and I was about to apologise for not asking permission to use the library for my research when he surprised me with an offer.

"How many have you written? We'd like to buy them off you."

It transpired that, following the great success *Trivial Pursuit* was enjoying worldwide, board games companies were rushing to release trivia games in time for the next Christmas, and the US giant MB (Milton Bradley) Games had approached *TV Times* about producing a branded game with them. The only problem was that there was very little time to compile the 2000 questions required.

I had my mind set on my TV trivia appearing in a book, with my name on the spine, but, aware that I was using *TV Times'* resources to compile my tome, I felt I had to engage in some kind of discussion about the project.

I agreed to meet with MB Games at their bright spacious southwest London offices, and it became obvious very quickly that the money on offer for the questions was a considerable sum. Negotiations were, therefore, going well when I submitted my final request, that my name should be included on the packaging stating that I had devised the questions.

"I'm sorry," said the company executive, smiling, "we can't offer you that – even the inventor of *Monopoly* doesn't have his name on the box."

I smiled back. "Then I'm sorry, we don't have a deal. No

name, no questions."

He continued to argue that naming credits were not customary in the board game industry, and I continued to hold firm on my assertion.

The meeting ended without agreement, and my thoughts turned to the discussion I would have to have with Eddie regarding gaining *TV Times'* blessing for me to publish my work in a book.

When I returned to the office, Eddie was surprised by my stance regarding MB Games, but didn't seem to be planning to block the publication of the book, for which, it's worth mentioning, I had still to find a publisher.

The following day, I received a call from my contact at MB Games conceding the namecheck on the packaging and agreeing the fee we had discussed. I was over the moon. Now all I had to do was write more than a thousand additional questions to a very tight deadline.

Working lunchtimes, nights and weekends, however, I completed the 2000 questions. When the first board game arrived in the office, I quickly opened it and looked at the inside of the box lid. There, in very small type, it stated "Questions devised by Colin Tough".

I swelled with pride; I'd outplayed the guy who invented *Monopoly*!

The game was a top seller in Christmas 1985 and every once in a while one pops up for sale on ebay.

I eventually wrote a small TV quiz book, published under the *TV Times* branding, but my next lunchtime project was on an altogether bigger scale.

It began one evening after Chris and I had been to see the musical *La Cage aux Folles* at the London Palladium theatre and met Ian and Janette in The Beehive after the show. Ian had spent the afternoon with an executive at the BBC discussing a new Krankies project, and he had told Ian that both BBC and ITV were planning to ramp up their daytime programming and were looking for new ideas. They were particularly interested in developing quiz shows, which were quick and relatively inexpensive to produce.

It got Ian and I discussing what made a good quiz show.

"Well," I said, thinking out loud, "it has to be about a subject that everyone has a certain amount of knowledge of, but which it's possible to develop a much deeper expertise in." I thought for a little longer and, with the evening's theatre visit freshly in mind, suggested, "Like stage and screen musicals."

"Great idea," said Ian. "Why don't you devise one?"

Emboldened by the evening's alcohol intake, and with a promise from Ian to present the format to his BBC contact, I concluded that was an excellent idea and promised to set to work the following day.

Next morning, however, as is so often the case with drink-fuelled notions, the idea held less appeal and it was quickly forgotten.

A few weeks later, I had lunch with Ian's agent, Stan Dallas. A former member of the sixties pop group The Dallas Boys, Stan was great company, and whenever possible we would meet up at a wine bar near his Regent Street office for a catch-up lunch.

Stan mentioned he'd had a call that morning from an ITV executive, Paul Stewart Laing, asking if any of his clients could suggest formats for daytime series, as the network was planning to increase its afternoon programming. I told Stan about my conversation with Ian, and he encouraged me to develop my thoughts further.

With an agent to represent me, I had no excuse, so I began to spend my weekday lunchtimes working on my musical quiz. Over the next few weeks, I devised the structure of the series and wrote a complete set of questions for one show.

Printing it out in the office and inserting it in a black

plastic binder from Rymans, I presented the package to Stan, more in hope than expectation.

Stan sent the proposal off to Paul Stewart Laing, who was head of programmes at TSW, one of the smallest ITV regions, which served the Southwest of England and had only won its franchise a few years earlier.

Months went by and, despite Stan encouraging me to be patient, I assumed the idea had gone no further than Paul's desk in Plymouth. Then out of the blue came the news that ITV had commissioned a pilot, a not-for-broadcast standalone one-off show to test the viability of the series.

The quiz got a name, *Sounds Like Music*, and a host, pianist and entertainer Bobby Crush, who had found fame winning the TV talent series *Opportunity Knocks* in the early seventies.

A few months later, we flew from London to Plymouth to watch the pilot being shot. Filmed with as little expense as possible, a strange set had been constructed with pillars that brought to mind the inside of a Roman temple, a desk for the presenter, Bobby, and opposite him a second longer desk, behind which sat the three contestants.

Normally a confident extrovert performer, often compared to a young Liberace, even before he played the American star in London's West End, Bobby came across as nervous and hesitant and the pilot felt rather flat. My hopes of a series being commissioned were not high, as we waited several more months for ITV to decide whether *Sounds Like Music* had a future.

To my amazement, the series got the green light and we returned to Plymouth to watch the first two shows being recorded. Bobby's performance the second time around was vastly improved, and he got better with every episode.

The series was a hit, often winning better audience appreciation figures than the top-rating primetime soap *Coronation Street*. It was commissioned for a second series, helped I have no doubt, given the subject matter and the camp presenter, by a more-than-average gay viewership.

Not everyone was as appreciative of the series, however. The *Evening Standard*'s acerbic TV reviewer Jaci Stephens summed it up as, "The quiz itself is fairly easy. If you answer Oscar Hammerstein every time, you will at least reach the final. It really is the pits. Crush certainly has charm and the camera likes him, but it's sad to see such a talented young man wasting his time here."

The entire review was cutting but very funny, so it was hard to take offence. I was just happy that the viewing public seemed to love the series, and in the end it ran for almost 50 shows. After I signed over the initial idea, there was nothing else for me to do but bank the cheques, which in total amounted to just short of £10,000, the equivalent of around £20,000 today.

While my extracurricular work was going well in the second half of the eighties, at *TV Times* I'd experienced one of the most embarrassing moments in my career and a development that taught me much about how *not* to manage a team.

I'd been asked to take over editing the magazine's listings pages for Channel 4, at the time a relatively new channel that had been added to the magazine when it launched the previous year. The channel was national, so unlike the regional schedules, its pages appeared in every edition of the magazine. Initially, I shared the pages with a second sub-editor but very quickly they became my sole charge.

The specific problem began with indecision at Channel 4. As part of its launch, the company had set up Channel 4 Films, which backed a large number of UK films, giving it the rights to premiere them exclusively on the channel.

One of its biggest releases to date, *Another Country*, a film loosely based on the life of Soviet spy Guy Burgess, was due to be screened on the channel on the Thursday evening of the issue I was working on, but Channel 4 was undecided as to what time to broadcast the film.

The normal practice when this occurred was to send down the rest of the day's programme schedule to the printers and to send the film synopsis and cast as a separate sheet of paper without any time, so that the two would be combined at the last minute when Channel 4 could confirm the exact starting time of the film.

Somehow, however, on this occasion there had been a miscommunication between me and the printers, and some degree of ambiguity had crept into the final pass of the pages, leaving it unclear whether the film started at 9.00 pm or 9.30 pm. Unbeknown to me, someone at the printers had taken it upon themselves to add the later time to the film, and that was what was published in the magazine.

The error went unnoticed until the day after the film was broadcast, at which point the complaints began to roll in by phone, by mail and by fax. With a circulation of more than 2.6 million, there were an awful lot of unhappy viewers and readers who wanted to register their anger at missing the start of the week's big film, which had begun at 9.00 pm.

The problem was accentuated by the fact that in 1987 there was a choice of just four channels in the UK, that *Another Country* was much anticipated, having been well received by the cinema critics, and, worst of all, that the film's star Rupert Everett was on the cover of *TV Times* that week, the very first time a Channel 4 programme had been awarded such an honour.

The film was screened on a Thursday evening. Since we didn't work on a Friday, it wasn't until the following Monday morning that I heard the news. I was mortified and sick to my stomach but that was nothing compared to the shame I felt at lunchtime.

As most of my colleagues began evacuating the office for their daily drinking or shopping expeditions, the editor's PA appeared. I watched as she began neatly attaching handwritten letters to the long wall that stretched the full length of the editorial floor.

I got up from my desk to take a closer look and realised that these were correspondence from irate readers who had written to complain about the listings error. As she continued to attach the letters to the wall, the PA apologised and assured me she was only following orders. But as lunchtime progressed, more and more letters were pinned on the wall until suddenly she stopped and began to reverse the process, taking the messages back down.

It transpired that another of the magazine's executives had contacted Channel 4 to apologise and had told them that the wall of complaints was being constructed to illustrate to me and my fellow subs the effect an error in the magazine could have on our readers. Word had then filtered through to the team I dealt with at the channel, and they had objected strenuously, praising the work I'd been doing over the past year, and demanding the letters be removed.

While even at the time I could see what the editor had set out to do with the exercise, I never forgot the wretchedness I felt. It taught me a huge leadership lesson, and I vowed that if I was ever in a management position, I'd never subject a member of my team to such humiliation.

My involvement with the team at Channel 4 worked to my advantage in another way a few years later, when it brought about a job offer.

Out of the blue, I received a call from a headhunting company, who explained they were recruiting for a role they felt might interest me. I found out later that my name had been passed to the headhunters by one of my contacts at Channel 4.

Intrigued, I supplied them with some details about my career to date and discovered the company they were recruiting for was a national newspaper. After a series of two or three phone calls, where we discussed my abilities, interests and ambitions, the caller revealed to me that the newspaper was *The Times,* and that the editor would like to meet me for breakfast.

I was gobsmacked. While I read *The Times,* I had always felt I was more of a tabloid journalist, and my experience of working on national newspapers was limited to the tabloid giants *The Sun* and *The News of the World.*

This, however, was an opportunity not to be missed. Arrangements were made to meet at The Savoy hotel one morning the following week. It was a daunting prospect, but I felt less intimidated when I realised that the paper's editor was Charlie Wilson, a former Royal Marines boxing champion from Glasgow, rather than the crusty public school William Rees Mogg, father of Conservative politician Jacob, who Charlie had succeeded a few years earlier.

Charlie had a reputation as a fiery pugnacious editor, who *Private Eye* magazine claimed once threw a reporter's typewriter out of the window because he didn't like what he was writing. He had been the husband of fellow journalist Anne Robinson, who went on to host *The Weakest Link* and *Countdown,* in what must have been a very turbulent marriage.

As I made my way along the London Embankment that morning, it seemed totally surreal – the editor of *The Times* and me having breakfast at The Savoy.

I was shown to a table by a head waiter, and a few minutes later I heard my name being called and turned to see Charlie Wilson's smiling face.

We began chatting and it soon became obvious we had a lot in common, other than our shared West of Scotland background. Like mine, Charlie's father had died when Charlie was very young. We had both wanted to be a journalist from an early age and we'd both gained places at

Glasgow University, only to turn them down to start at the bottom in newspapers.

At the time of the breakfast, I was acting deputy chief sub-editor on *TV Times*, covering a maternity leave, and some months earlier I'd covered another maternity leave as deputy head of forward planning, a job I loved as it meant travelling around the various ITV regions discussing upcoming series with heads of programming.

When, towards the end of what was a very enjoyable breakfast conversation, Charlie revealed that the job he was interviewing me for was chief features sub on *The Times*, I was totally amazed. He promised to be in touch, and I walked back towards Embankment station in a complete and utter daze.

A couple of days later, I got a call from Michael Hoy, managing editor of *The Times*. "We're delighted to be able to offer you the position as chief sub-editor on *The Times* at a salary of £31,000 a year," he told me. Almost immediately then asking, "When can you start?"

I was a little taken aback by his presumption that I would instantly want the job and slightly put off by what appeared to be a corporate arrogance that no one would turn down *The Times* of London. I explained that I would obviously have to discuss the offer with my partner, Chris, and he, rather reluctantly it appeared to me, granted me a couple of days to come back to him.

I talked over the job offer with Chris and mentioned it to a couple of colleagues at *TV Times*, including the deputy editor, Frank Walker. His reaction was similar to most others, who believed it was too good an offer to reject.

"Once you've held a senior position at *The Times*, particularly at a young age, you're set up for life," he suggested.

I still had nagging doubts. I felt my journalistic skills were much more aligned with tabloid newspapers, like *The Sun* and *The Mirror*, and that a move to a broadsheet may be a mistake. In addition, I had been working on a research dummy for a new TV magazine that was being considered as a possible sister title for *TV Times* and I was hoping, if it was launched, that I would get a senior role on the team.

I wrestled with *The Times'* offer for a couple of days and finally decided to turn it down, but as well as writing to Michael Hoy to inform him of my decision, I also took the time to send a message to Charlie Wilson, explaining my decision in light of the research work I was employed in and assuring him I was honoured to have been offered the role on his paper.

He replied with a pleasant letter, saying, "Many thanks for your note. I appreciate the reason you outlined and I wish you and your new project the best of luck. Perhaps we may have another opportunity some time in the future."

Charlie Wilson's reply had an eerie hint of clairvoyance as our paths were to cross again less than six months later.

# CHAPTER 10

It became obvious a few months after we put the dummy TV magazine into research that a launch was not imminent, and so I went back to my normal day job. In January 1989, however, an unexpected opportunity arose.

I was contacted by Murdoch Magazines and offered a role that combined my love of journalism with my fascination for technology. The company, which was the magazine arm of Rupert Murdoch's News Corp organisation, had decided that instead of employing a multitude of contributors to compile the daily listings for its UK newspapers, the TV schedules could be written and stored on a computer database that could spit out the TV pages in the required styles for each publication.

There was also a strong drive, supported by Murdoch and other publishers, to change the archaic laws that supported the TV listings duopoly, whereby *Radio Times* had the sole rights to print BBC weekly listings and only *TV Times* could publish ITV and Channel 4 seven-day schedules. Murdoch believed a database-driven listings operation would give him a huge editorial advantage when the time came, and that he could publish a multi-channel weekly TV magazine.

He had bought the American magazine *TV Guide*, then the biggest-selling magazine in the world, and had launched a UK version. The British title was at the time limited to publishing TV listings for his recently launched Sky satellite channels and a small selection of daily highlights for the four terrestrial channels. However, the plan was to include full BBC, ITV and Channel 4 schedules as soon as the law allowed.

I was interviewed for the job at the company's classy

offices in London's Haymarket by Murdoch Magazines' managing director, a stylish lady, small in stature but big in personality, who sported the decade's power-woman outfit of bouffant hair and shoulder pads.

We discussed the job, the innovative aspect of which had an immediate appeal for me, and as we parted, she promised to be in touch. When I returned to the office, I felt I wanted to discuss the opportunity with someone, and mentioned it to the chief sub, Paul Parish. To my astonishment, Paul revealed that he had been approached about the job before me and that negotiations had reached an advanced stage before he had admitted to himself that the job wasn't for him.

The following day, I received a call from the Murdoch Magazines MD offering me the job and outlining the package on offer. Thanking her and promising I'd get back to her with an answer quickly, the moment I got off the phone I immediately discussed the deal with Paul. He told me that in his negotiations he'd raised the salary twice before finally rejecting the offer.

It was an invaluable piece of information. I've never been good at negotiating a deal when I really want something; job satisfaction was much more important to me than money and the idea that I might lose an opportunity because I'd pushed the pay too high always acted as a brake on my bargaining. The information Paul had shared with me, however, meant I knew exactly what Murdoch Magazines were willing to pay.

I called the MD, and told her how excited I was about the job but that I felt the remuneration for the role should be higher and stated my price. After a short lecture about her desire to recruit someone who really wanted the job and wasn't just after a large payday, she acquiesced and we agreed a deal.

Strangely, that same day *TV Times* was sold by

Independent Television Publications, a company wholly owned by the ITV companies, to magazine giants IPC Magazines, publishers of *Woman, Woman's Own, Women's Weekly* and a host of other best-selling titles, with an eye to the ending of the TV listings duopoly that seemed inevitable.

The job title I'd been given was TV Database Manager, hardly the most journalistic title I remember thinking, but what did the title matter? This was an exciting new project, and I was building it from the ground up.

It was only when I arrived at Rupert Murdoch's huge Wapping headquarters that I realised the expectations were that I would have some degree of database management skills, something that had never been discussed in my interviews with the MD. I suspect that her understanding of what the role involved was fairly limited and that led to her confining the interview process to areas she felt comfortable to discuss.

When in my first week the language being used at meetings revolved around SQL and BASIC more than columns and pages, I knew I was in trouble. I found a saviour in a lovely man called Richard Withey. He was a librarian in charge of building an archive database for *The Times* and he put an arm around my shoulder and helped me through the initial few months of tech talk.

Until the TV listings duopoly was dismantled and Murdoch could launch a multi-channel TV guide, the TV listings database would exclusively serve the News Corp UK newspapers – *The Sun, The News of the World, The Times, The Sunday Times* and *Today*, the UK's first full-colour newspaper which closed in 1995. Those five newspapers would also be expected to shoulder the cost of the operation I was setting up, so a meeting with the five newspaper editors was arranged for the boardroom at News Corp's Wapping HQ.

My MD and I were both nervous when we arrived for

the meeting, as we knew the editors were not keen to hand over control of key pages of their newspapers to a third party that would be charging them for the service.

For a young journalist, not yet 30, it was an intimidating event to be sitting around a table with five of the most revered editors in the country, aware that what was to follow could well involve me having to justify my new role to them.

The group included Kelvin Mackenzie, infamous editor of *The Sun*, who was known for his brutal tongue and who during the exchange rate crisis in 1992 told the then prime minister John Major, "Well, John, let me put it this way. I've got a large bucket of shit lying on my desk and tomorrow morning I'm going to pour it all over your head."

Also in attendance was the fearsome Charlie Wilson, editor of *The Times* and the man whose job offer I'd rejected just five months earlier. How was he going to react to me turning him down, and soon after, joining another wing of the News Corp organisation.

The meeting's chairman Sir Edward Pickering entered the room. Almost 80 and a commanding presence, Sir Edward was a former editor of the *Daily Express*. In his time there, he had acted as a mentor to the young Rupert Murdoch, who worked as a sub-editor in the fifties to gain experience of the newspaper world. Murdoch had developed a father-son relationship with the man he called "Pick". He appointed Sir Edward as executive vice-chairman of News International, the British subsidiary of his News Corp global operation in 1981.

Very quickly the meeting became heated, with the newspaper editors, as expected, pointing out that not only did they not want to relinquish control of their TV pages to a separate entity but they were also unwilling to fund the operation. The argument raged around the table, with all the editors united in their rejection of the services the team I was recruiting was being employed to provide.

The MD struggled to put forward the case for the new TV database unit, but her positive arguments were drowned out by the cacophony of the five editors.

My heart sank as I considered that the career move I'd so recently made may have been both ill-conceived and short lived, until Sir Edward held up his hand to stop the largely one-sided discussion.

"What does Rupert want?" he asked quietly.

My MD was quick to reply. "He wants a TV database team to feed the newspapers and *TV Guide*," she said confidently.

"Then that is the end of the argument," responded Sir Edward, and that was that.

The discussion changed from whether the unit should be set up to how it should be paid for by the individual papers. I had witnessed the strength of an organisation that is run by one man with a vision, who has the first and the last word on all aspects of the business. It was a refreshing change to the prolonged executive stalemate I'd often seen operate in such circumstances in the past.

Throughout the meeting, I'd eyed Charlie Wilson across the huge boardroom table, conscious that our history might have made him resentful that I had rejected his job offer and then quickly jumped ship from *TV Times* to join this new unit that he was so opposed to.

After the meeting ended, having left my boss so she could discuss the outcome with Sir Edward, I found myself standing next to Charlie as I pressed the lift button to return to the ground floor. I gave a nod of acknowledgement. Filling the silence as we travelled down, I mumbled something about being sorry I hadn't been able to take up his offer. I instantly wished I hadn't, as it came out as a garbled mess.

Leaving the lift on the ground floor, Charlie gave me a playful smile. "Just to let you know, if you'd taken the chief sub's job, you'd be my features editor by now."

I watched as he walked off towards the converted warehouse that housed *The Times* and *The Sunday Times*, unsure whether his parting words were merely voiced as a form of payback for my rejection of his offer or whether I genuinely had turned down a role that would have led to me becoming features editor of *The Times*.

Charlie Wilson and I were undoubtedly a good fit for each other and it's possible that with similar backgrounds and attitudes to journalism he had seen something of himself in me. Just a few months after our conversation in the lift, however, Simon Jenkins replaced him in the chair at *The Times*. Jenkins' background – boarding school and Oxford – couldn't have been further removed from mine, so if I had found myself in a senior editorial role on the paper, it may well not have lasted for long.

In the following months, I began to build my TV listings team, recruiting eager young journalists, including TV reviewer and later *Heat* TV Editor Boyd Hilton, who was starting out in his career.

The team moved to an office on the west side of Leicester Square, a wonderful buzzy location with only one drawback. My office was directly opposite and level with the Swiss glockenspiel clock in the Swiss Centre at the entrance to the square. On the hour, the clock's 11 Swiss figures would rotate and its 27 huge bells would chime for two minutes, deafening everyone in the office and making conversation totally impossible.

I've mentioned the *TV Times-Radio Times* duopoly a number of times and, while it was very much in my interests that the arrangement should continue while I worked for *TV Times*, the opposite was now the case, as Rupert Murdoch had huge plans for his publications when it ended.

To recap, at the start of the 1990s, if you wanted to have a complete picture of the week's TV schedules for the four

TV channels available to most of the UK – BBC1, BBC2, ITV and Channel 4 – you needed to buy both the *Radio Times*, for the BBC channels, and *TV Times*, for the two commercial channels. The daily newspapers were allowed to publish TV listings for all channels, but only for the day of publication. Weekly and weekend papers could print Saturday and Sunday listings. Magazines and newspapers could publish a limited number of previews of programmes on a weekly basis but not enough to allow readers to use them as a listings guide.

In 1982, using the launch of Channel 4 as a justification, Tony Elliott, the publisher of London entertainment guide *Time Out*, exploited the fact that his publication's printing deadline came after the two TV magazines were already in the shops. He copied listings from them and printed them in his London magazine *Time Out*. Tony lost a subsequent court case brought against him, but his campaign was boosted a couple of years later when the Office of Fair Trading concluded that the duopoly was against the public interest.

Cracks had begun to appear in the restrictions but the BBC, which owned *Radio Times*, and the ITV companies, which at the time owned *TV Times*, continued to fight on.

Tony formed a group of publishers to campaign for an end to the duopoly. I was asked to represent Rupert Murdoch's publications, along with Jane Reed, News International's corporate affairs director and formerly a distinguished women's magazine editor.

I found myself playing the role of gamekeeper-turned-poacher and became heavily involved in the campaign to overturn the listings duopoly.

Despite working long hours setting up the listings bureau and campaigning with Tony's pressure group, Chris and I still found time for holidays, regularly hiring boats on the

French waterways. We were also making regular twice-yearly visits to Scotland to see family and friends. In between, my mother, Betty, would make the journey down to London to stay in Ian and Janette's flat below ours.

As I've explained, my mother had always been a bit of a snob. I know she enjoyed regaling her friends at church with tales of her trips to see her journalist son in London and her various excursions to see Ian and Janette in pantomime at Christmas or in one of their summer seasons at a British seaside resort.

Strangely, she tried, successfully for a time, to drive a wedge between me and my older brother, Alistair. Knowing we saw little of each other, particularly after I moved to London, she would feed each of us stories about the other, designed to encourage ill feeling between us.

Whether she would have attempted the same with me and Ian had we not been so close, both personally and geographically, I've no idea, but it was a strange inclination for a mother to attempt to sow seeds of distrust between two of her children.

Her pride in the success that Ian and Janette had achieved as The Krankies, on the other hand, led to her name dropping in a quite shameless fashion, a habit that resulted in an embarrassing moment one festive season.

Mum was visiting Ian and Janette during a pantomime run at the Theatre Royal in Newcastle when they were invited to appear in a big charity show one Sunday at the theatre. With nothing else to do on a bleak January Sunday afternoon in the Northeast, Betty tagged along to rehearsals with them as they ran through their act at the theatre.

Standing alone in the wings, she noticed an old man in a shabby raincoat idly tapping out a tune on the grand piano that sat to one side of the stage. She sidled over to where he sat and began to engage him in conversation.

"I'm Ian of The Krankies' mother," she began by stating

proudly. "I'm down from Scotland for the pantomime."

He smiled and told her he was looking forward to watching their act that evening.

"Are you performing tonight?" she asked, and he replied that he was playing a small part in the proceedings.

"So, what is it you do?" she wondered, pushing on further with her inquisition.

"I'm an actor," replied the old man, as he continued to pick out notes on the keyboard.

Intrigued by his answer, Mum continued her probing. "Would I have seen you much on TV?" she asked.

"I've not done a great deal of TV," he admitted.

Just then, Ian appeared at the side of the stage and called her over.

"Lovely to meet you," said Mum as she headed towards the wings. "I do hope you manage to get some TV work in the coming year."

As she reached Ian, he looked anxiously at her and back towards the old man at the piano. "What on earth have you been talking to Sir John about?" he asked, a look of panic in his eyes.

"Sir John?" Mum replied, puzzled.

"Yes, that's Sir John Mills," Ian explained, ushering her away from the stage.

Mum had wished one of Britain's greatest-ever film actors, who had chosen to shun television for most of his career, good luck in picking up some TV roles in the mistaken belief that he was a down-at-heel out-of-work thespian.

Later that night, after the show, Ian had his own embarrassing moment with Sir John when, at the post-show party, after a great deal of alcohol had been consumed by all concerned, sitting on a bar stool next to the great man Ian admitted that as a schoolboy he'd had a crush on Sir

John's actress daughter, Hayley.

"Ah," said the theatrical legend, lifting his glass in salute. "I'll be seeing her next week. I'll let her know."

Around the same time, Mum had another mortifying moment when she visited Ian and Janette during a summer season in Bournemouth.

That summer, Ian and Janette were living on their boat, a beautiful trawler-style Grand Banks yacht in Poole marina. One Sunday, Mum, Ian and Janette, and their bass player, Harvey Smith, had all set off for a day's sailing and Sunday lunch at sea.

An hour or so out into the English Channel, Ian nipped downstairs from the flybridge, where everyone was enjoying the sunshine, to check the progress of the roast dinner. He discovered the cabin was filling with water and the boat was sinking.

He later learned that one of the nearby boats in the marina had incorrectly hooked up their electrical supply, resulting in a chemical reaction that led over time to surrounding boats being stripped of all their metal. That day, this had led to the perishing of a metal seal that was holding the depth finder on the underside of the boat, allowing water to flood in.

Ian immediately called the coastguard. A lifeboat was sent out to rescue the quartet, pulling the 36-foot Grand Banks up onto the nearest beach. It just so happened, however, that the closest landmass to the incident was at Sandbanks – the largest nudist beach in the UK.

Betty was mortified, as she came ashore and walked from the boat through the crowds of curious naturists on the sandy beach towards the sanctuary of a waiting car.


Mum was very spritely well into her 80s and would regularly visit us in Surrey. However, after a fall while visiting Alistair and his family in Rothesay, her health began to deteriorate – although not quite as quickly as I had first imagined.

After the tumble in which she damaged her hip, Betty was taken across on the ferry from Rothesay to Inverclyde Royal on the Scottish mainland, the nearest hospital to the island, which sits on a hill overlooking the river Clyde outside the town of Greenock.

I couldn't get up to Scotland immediately, so I called regularly for updates and was put through to a phone by Betty's bedside. The second time I called, she seemed fairly with-it but something she said set warning bells ringing.

"I've had a lovely day," she told me. "This afternoon I watched the QE2 sailing up the Clyde past the hospital."

I came off the phone crestfallen and, relating the story about the QE2, warned Chris that I feared Mum's mind was beginning to go. "She's obviously thinking back to the day she attended the ship's launch with my dad back in 1967," I concluded sadly.

The next day, however, I decided to do some checking before letting Ian and Alistair know my fears, and nipped into my local travel agent shop to check exactly where in the world the QE2 was the previous day. I requested a brochure for the ship from the assistant and checked its itinerary for the day in question. Amazingly, it was on a journey around the coast of the United Kingdom and that day had docked in Greenock. So much for my theory that Mum was beginning to suffer some form of dementia.

Mum was released from hospital a few weeks later and, after a short spell in a convalescent home, was soon back in her own house in Clydebank. Soon after we visited her, once again I erroneously worried about her welfare.

Chris, Alexander and I had arrived early in the evening at her bungalow, climbed the steps to her front door and dropped off our cases. We had a brief chat before rushing across the Drumry Road to see my Uncle Bobby and Aunt

Betty before Alexander's bedtime.

When we returned, we found Betty lying on the floor, her glasses broken, nursing a nasty bump on the head. Her mobility having become impaired since her fall, she had tripped over the suitcases in the gloomy hallway and hit her head as she fell.

Chris led her into the lounge, and I went to the kitchen to get something out of the freezer to reduce the swelling that was beginning to appear over her left eye. Grabbing a frozen package, I returned to the lounge to find Chris staunching the blood that was trickling down Mum's face.

I placed the frozen package on the wound, and we chatted to Mum, who was fairly calm about the whole incident. It was then I began to worry about whether she had been taking care of herself since she'd returned home. I knew major changes to routine, such as the time Betty had spent in hospital and rehabilitation, could result in older people neglecting areas such as personal care and hygiene and I was now aware of a very fishy stench emanating from Mum.

It struck me that I was going to be forced to have a very difficult conversation with her at some point during the visit. As we chatted, my hand holding the now rapidly defrosting package to her head, I began to consider whether it would be better for me or Chris to have this discussion. Then I looked up at what I was pressing above Mum's eye and let out a sudden laugh.

Chris was puzzled at my outburst but laughed along when I revealed the full story later. The pungent smell I could detect coming from Betty wasn't a lack of self-care but was the result of a swiftly defrosting slab of haddock that I had used to minimise the bruising above her eye.

Unfortunately, those early worries about Mum's state of mind, although unfounded, did precede her eventual decline following that fall, resulting in her being admitted to a Clydebank nursing home, where she eventually died at the age of 93.

# CHAPTER 11

By the summer of 1990, the TV database had proved a success for News International. As an end to the listings duopoly appeared to be increasingly likely, I was more and more involved in the plans to develop the UK edition of *TV Guide* as a competitor to *Radio Times* and *TV Times*.

*TV Guide* had been launched with Sky listings and BBC, ITV and Channel 4 highlights by editor Ian Birch. Ian had previously very successfully launched *Sky*, a youth entertainment magazine that despite sharing its name was totally unconnected to the TV business, for Rupert Murdoch in 1987. When Murdoch announced plans for a TV magazine, Ian had been the obvious choice to edit it.

Murdoch's plan was to slowly build circulation by featuring Sky TV channel listings until the time that *TV Times* and *Radio Times* lost their exclusivity, at which point it could launch against them, from an existing solid sales base.

In June 1990, Ian decided he wanted to explore other journalistic opportunities and resigned as editor of *TV Guide*. The MD immediately called me into her office and offered me the job. While I hadn't ever considered a roadmap for my career, never mind set out any timetable, I was thrilled to be asked to edit my first magazine before I was 30, having taken the chair at my first newspaper at the age of just 19.

Chris and I had decided to get married in 1990. "It's a nice, neat round number," she had concluded when we had discussed a possible date for our nuptials. It was only in jest that I suggested 2000 was even neater. That said, the simplicity of the date has done nothing for my ability to recall how many years we've been married when asked in the decades since.

Arrangements for the big day were in place when I

returned home the evening of my chat with the MD.

"I've got some good news, and some bad news," I revealed to Chris as I came through the door of the flat. "The good news is I'm going to edit *TV Guide*; the bad news is we've got to cancel our honeymoon."

Chris was as thrilled with the news of my new role as I was and agreed that, in the bigger picture, putting off our post-wedding trip was a small price to pay.

We were married at Marylebone Town Hall with a small number of friends and family attending the ceremony. As we left the building, we walked under an impressive arch of tennis rackets held aloft by players in pristine white shorts and T-shirts. It made a perfect photo, even if the players had raised their rackets for the wrong couple, their intended targets following us out of the building a few minutes later.

We had lunch in a local Paddington restaurant with our closest family members and then a celebratory party at London Zoo, with a large group of guests. We'd been warned not to wander out from the function rooms into the zoo itself, but the waitresses assured us that, while the guidance was for health and safety purposes, they'd never had a party follow those instructions.

Such as has always been my fascination with the animals that I spent most of my wedding evening ferrying groups of guests out to visit the residents of the park – in particular, a gorilla who would slowly raise his head each time he heard the distant sound of laughter approaching his enclosure, only to return to his slumbers when he saw it was just me with another group of drunken revellers.

Having cancelled our honeymoon, due to my new job, I'd arranged to stay in a lovely country house hotel near Windsor the day after the wedding and have a special meal at the world-famous Waterside Inn. It became the first restaurant outside France to hold three Michelin stars for 25 years. We had visited once before, for a special Sunday

180

lunch deal, with Joy and Stuart, friends from The Beehive. That second evening of our marriage, however, we were planning to eat from the à la carte menu, a huge treat… and a huge expense for us at the time!

Despite the constant trips out to talk to the animals at the wedding party, I still managed to consume a fair amount of booze that night, resulting in a huge hangover that refused to shift as the following day progressed. The perfect meal at the perfect restaurant was unfortunately far from it but the wedding itself was an unforgettable occasion.

Memories of my first few months as *TV Guide* editor were not nearly as pleasant as my recollections of our big day. Ian Birch had been a very charismatic leader and many of the staff, some of whom had followed him from *Sky* magazine, were unhappy working for a new untested boss.

To be honest, I was far from assured when I took on that first magazine editorship and tended to have more confidence in my team members than I did in my own ability. This resulted in page layouts and articles going straight into the magazine, with very little intervention from me.

After a few weeks, I realised I needed to stamp my authority and gathered the renegade members of the team to tell them I had no intention of going anywhere and if they weren't happy with me leading the team their only alternative was to leave. Some took my advice, while others took the decision to nail their colours to my mast. The air had been cleared and we were now ready to begin to plan for the battle ahead.

I introduced a number of innovations to *TV Guide* as we prepared it to take on the big two listings guides when the now-inevitable ending of the duopoly was announced. Some, like colour-coding the channels, were later adopted by our competitors. Others were more radical, such as printing the listings section as a smaller page size on a different paper stock in the centre of the magazine, to make it easier to turn straight to the TV schedules.

The changes were a success and sales began to climb, delivering me my first nomination for a prestigious British Society of Magazine Editors (BSME) award.

The awards ceremony was held at the huge Grosvenor House Hotel in Park Lane and the great and the good of the magazine business, at the time a thriving successful industry, enjoyed a three-course meal and a great deal of wine and champagne.

I had often seen Grosvenor House's Great Room, one of the largest function rooms in the UK, on TV, as it was home to many major events in the second half of the 20th century, from Miss World contests to BAFTA Award ceremonies. Huge screens flanked the stage, allowing everyone wherever they were in the room to see the unfolding events.

When it came to the category I was nominated in, General Interest Magazines (Weekly), my name was announced along with the other nominees, and our faces were displayed on the gigantic screens above the audience. I sat, poker-faced, as members of the publishing team around the table smiled supportively. A few tables away, I could see my former colleagues from *TV Times* eying our table expectantly.

My heart was racing as, Oscar-style, the envelope was opened.

"And the winner is," said the presenter, "the editor of an innovative TV listings title…"

There was a pause, and in that tiny moment, I did the most embarrassing thing possible. I looked around the table and opened my mouth in disbelief at my success, just in time to hear the winner announced as "Nicholas Brett of the *Radio Times*".

To lose was no disgrace but to have celebrated victory, only to discover a major competitor was in fact the winner, was humiliating. I was nominated 15 more times for a BSME award but never made the same mistake again.

Towards the end of 1990, the MD was asked to visit the offices of American *TV Guide*, still at the time the biggest-selling magazine on the planet, in the States to present our plans for the UK edition once the TV listings market was deregulated and the duopoly was ended.

She had taken little interest in the editorial development of the title up until that point, having had much of her time taken up focussing on the more urgent launch of a new women's magazine called *Mirabella*. When she was asked to travel to Pennsylvania to discuss the future plans for the UK *TV Guide*, she decided at the last minute that she needed me to accompany her across the Atlantic.

When I say accompany her, I should point out that rather than travel with her on the same flight in British Airways business class, her PA made it plain that I would instead be travelling on a cheaper Virgin Atlantic plane later in the day. While relieved that I wouldn't have to make small talk with my boss on the eight-hour journey, having done a day's work before I even set off to the airport, I was exhausted by the time I reached the Big Apple.

Climbing into a taxi at JFK Airport, I instructed the driver to take me to the Royalton Hotel, just east of Times Square. My boss and I were due to set off early the following morning to catch the train from New York Penn Station to Pennsylvania, so to make arrangements simpler she had booked me into the hotel where she was staying. As I quickly learned from the driver, the Royalton was *the* place to stay in New York at the start of the nineties, having undergone a multi-million-dollar refurbishment just a couple of years earlier.

Walking through the grey-pillared entrance, I approached the small reception desk on the right to be met by a beaming clerk, who welcomed me with a camp flourish.

"Just a second, Mr Tough, while I check your room is ready," he cautioned me. This struck me as strange, as it was now nearly eleven o'clock at night.

He bashed away at a computer keyboard, looking more and more confused with every stroke. "I've just got a slight problem here," he confided, as he continued to type furiously.

"Please," I pleaded, "my body clock is telling me it's four in the morning. If you haven't got a room for me, I'd be happy to sleep in a store cupboard."

A few seconds later, he stopped typing and, smiling, returned his gaze to me. "Do we have a room for you, Mr Tough?" he purred slowly, as if he was about to pull a white rabbit out of his hat. "Follow me," he urged triumphantly, and we set off for the elevator.

The lift headed upwards until we reached the sixteenth floor. When the doors opened, my guide gestured for me to exit. A little way down the corridor, we came to a door, which he opened and held for me to walk in. Instead of the standard US hotel room, with a clothes closet on the left and a bathroom and toilet on the right leading on to the bedroom itself, I was puzzled to be confronted by yet another hallway.

"This," explained my camp companion with a proud theatrical wink, "is our presidential suite!"

The hallway was around thirty feet long, and displayed along the right-hand wall were a variety of ornaments in glass cabinets, like the lobby outside a hotel gift shop. At the end of the corridor, three steps led up to a raised dais with floor lights shooting up from it, reminiscent of the transporter room platform in *Star Trek.* Down three steps to the right of the dais was a huge dining table, at the centre of which was a vase holding more tulips than I could count. The dining room led to a stainless-steel kitchen larger than the one Chris and I had in our flat in Marylebone.

Down another set of steps to the left was a beautifully furnished lounge, with two leather settees, a coffee table, a large-screen TV, a DVD player and a huge library of discs. Leading off the lounge was a bedroom, with a bed that pulled down from the wall, and off that a gleaming chrome bathroom, large enough for a family of four to all use at the same time.

It was simply breathtaking.

I thanked the receptionist, palmed him a five-dollar tip, almost certainly the smallest gratuity ever offered by an occupant of the palace I was about to spend the night in, and, mindful of my early start, headed for bed.

Aware that I'd be arriving late in New York and that I wouldn't want to have to wait for room service to deliver me a meal before I could get to sleep, I'd asked Chris to buy me a Marks and Spencer tuna sandwich and a small one-glass bottle of Merlot that I could enjoy before lights out. As I sat on a chair in the bedroom munching my sandwich and swilling my wine, I considered the surprise the housekeeper would receive the following morning when she found the M&S sandwich packaging and plastic wine bottle in the bedroom bin.

I wished Chris was with me as tomorrow was Valentine's Day and this would have been the most romantic of venues. I eased between the sheets and stretched to switch off the light. Just a few minutes later, the phone rang. Startled, I jumped out of bed and sat on the edge of the mattress.

It was my buddy from reception. "Hello, Mr Tough, how are you?" he enquired. "Your boss has asked me to check that you are comfortable."

I told him I was very comfortable, asked him to thank her for her concern, hung up the phone and switched off the light.

Now, anyone who knows me will admit that I often have

an overactive imagination. It has in the past sometimes worked in my favour, like the night as an eight-year-old, when I visited the little post office around the corner from my home in Clydebank to buy a bar of chocolate and was told by an unfamiliar gruff voice that the shop was closed. Suspicious, I noted down the registration of the car outside the shop, so when the police discovered the owner, Mr Johnston, had been coshed and the post office raided, I managed to help the investigation.

On the occasion of my visit to the Royalton, however, my imagination rather ran away with me. Having first thought what a nice gesture it was for the MD to have enquired after my welfare, I then began to put two and two together and make a much larger number.

How strange, I thought, that I should have been given such a grand suite. Why would my MD contact the receptionist to ask about me? Had she planned this all along? She's a middle-aged woman and I'm barely 30. Has she set the whole thing up? Was this the way the corporate world worked?

The more my mind raced with my conspiracy theory, the more I became convinced it was true, and the more I worried she was about to turn up at the end of my hallway in a night dress and attempt to seduce me. What was I to do? I loved Chris and I wouldn't cheat on her for anyone.

It took a long time to get to sleep that night and I lost count of the number of times I was certain I could hear the front door of the suite creak open. I did, however, finally fall asleep and there was no midnight visitation. Where the notion had come from, I have no idea. My MD was always the most professional of bosses and hugely supportive to her team.

The Royalton had one more surprise for me. The following morning, I woke to the sound of my alarm and walked into the lounge. Naked, I climbed the three steps onto the dais and pressed the button to open the blinds to get my first daytime view of New York. As I stood there in my birthday suit, instead of the wonderful scene of Manhattan's skyline I'd expected from the sixteenth floor, what came into view was a busy office full of workers in the building directly across the narrow side street that housed the hotel. I hit the deck immediately and crawled along the floor and down the steps towards the safety of the bedroom and my clothes.

Early that morning, we set off to catch the shuttle train from New York to Radnor, Pennsylvania. It wasn't my first visit to Radnor, home of *TV Guide*, as I'd first made the trip just a few weeks after I joined Murdoch Magazines.

At the time, Rupert Murdoch had only just done the deal that bought the magazine from its previous owner, Walter Annenberg, the businessman and philanthropist who was also at one time the United States ambassador to the United Kingdom. Due to the extensive list of questions I fired at the team, my visit was treated with a great deal of suspicion, as they initially believed I was some kind of undercover agent working for the new owner. Once I explained that I too was new to the company and was simply attempting to learn how their successful operation had been developed, in order to build a UK version, I was treated with great kindness and made a number of good friends.

The *TV Guide* complex of buildings dominated the small town of Radnor. It was a huge operation that employed hundreds of members of staff in a number of buildings.

When my MD and I arrived, we were immediately shown to the boardroom and introduced to the magazine's senior executives. After a short preamble from my boss, reminding them that Murdoch's plan was to launch into the market as soon as the *Radio Times*-*TV Times* duopoly ended, it was over to me to present my plans for the UK magazine.

The US contingent listened politely as I presented my

vision of what the title would look like post-deregulation. While sticking largely to the format British readers were used to with the two existing TV magazines, it also introduced a number of innovative features.

Having heard my sell, the US executives thanked me and then metaphorically swept my plans off the table before physically placing the compact-sized *TV Guide* in front of me.

"That," they explained, "is how you design a TV magazine." They asserted that, as they were the biggest-selling magazine in the world, their way had to be the best and the only way.

The US magazine was set out in a very different fashion from the traditional UK listings. Whereas *TV Times* and *Radio Times* listed programmes by channels, allowing readers to view separate columns for each individual channel, each displaying programmes from early morning to late night, the US *TV Guide* listed programmes by time, showing all the shows starting at 8 pm, followed by the programmes beginning at 8.30 pm and so on. While it was the traditional way for US TV viewers to access the information, I knew it would be totally alien and confusing to British eyes.

This chronological method of displaying the information was augmented by a listings grid, similar to the way we now see schedules displayed on digital television electronic programme guides, something unheard of at the time in the UK.

I attempted to argue my corner, explaining that to introduce such a system for my readers would be akin to asking them to learn a new language; they would simply reject it and turn to a competitor title that offered a more traditional format.

My boss called a halt to the discussion, which was beginning to become somewhat heated, and she appeared to side with the American view as we left the building less than two hours after having arrived. She was going on to have a series of meetings to discuss *Mirabella*, and I headed back to New York by train alone, slightly dejected by the conversations I'd had in Pennsylvania.

I decided that as I had a little time before my plane's departure time, I'd visit Cafe Fiorello, a restaurant on Upper Broadway that Chris and I had eaten in during a previous visit to New York. The restaurant served a wonderful pie-style pizza that we both became addicted to, and it struck me as the perfect antidote to what had turned out to be a rather dispiriting trip.

As I left the ageing grandeur of Penn Station and began the half-hour walk up 8th Avenue, the heavens opened and, just minutes later, the strap on my luggage bag snapped. I was forced to carry it in the pelting rain, both hands clasped under it like a sack of King Edwards, as I attempted, unsuccessfully, to hail a yellow New York taxi with miniscule jerking movements of my right arm.

By the time I arrived at Fiorello's, I was soaked and aching but definitely ready for my pizza pie. I scanned the menu, but there was no sign of the mouth-watering delicacy.

"Do you have a separate menu for the pizza pies," I asked, water still dribbling down my nose from my sodden hair.

"I'm sorry," the waitress imparted, with a look of genuine regret, "we're currently only serving from our pre-theatre menu."

So it was that barely 24 hours after I'd originally left London, totally dispirited, drenched and with an aching back, I boarded my flight at JFK back to Heathrow. I had one priority in mind throughout the return journey. I had to discredit the idea that the *TV Guide* way was the only way, otherwise Murdoch's launch against *Radio Times* and *TV Times* was dead in the water.

That evening on the journey home, I devised a plan. I

189

was going to have to demonstrate to the Murdoch Magazines team why the US-style of TV listings wouldn't work in the UK, and that meant producing a live set of UK listings pages formatted like *TV Guide*.

I hired an Apple Mac, now the chosen workhorse for magazine production but at the time something of a novelty, and an expert designer. Together, we produced one weekend of UK listings, with the four terrestrial channels, plus channels from Sky and its competitor satellite service BSB. Working long hours all week, we had the package complete by Friday lunchtime.

The pages were then carefully slotted into plastic folders and that afternoon distributed to all the members of staff working at the company's Haymarket HQ to use over the following two days.

As I handed the MD her copy, she informed me that unfortunately she wouldn't be able to take part in the test, as she was flying to Paris for the weekend, but that she would pass it on to her husband to use. My heart dropped. The most important person whose opinion I was attempting to influence wasn't even going to be in the country that weekend.

The following Monday, the reaction to the US-style listings was an overwhelming thumbs down. Everyone had found them confusing to use but I still wasn't certain that the staff's response would trump the trust my boss had in the Americans' guidance. I entered her spacious office and took a seat, and was about to reel off a well-rehearsed speech about the horrendous experiences I'd been told about by my colleagues, when she cut me off.

"Well," she said. "Before I left for Paris, I binned all the TV guides and papers in the house and left my husband with your TV guide folder. When I got back, he told me he'd returned from having a few drinks on a night out and almost put his foot through the TV in frustration as he

190

attempted to find out what he could watch."

The battle was won and the US approach was ditched.

My trips to *TV Guide* in Radnor, Pennsylvania, were not my first visits to the United States, and they were far from my last. A couple of years after my dad died, relatives in America invited me and my mother to visit them in Massachusetts and New Jersey, and we spent three weeks in the summer of 1976 as the country celebrated its bicentennial.

Soon after my first visit to Radnor, Chris and I decided to make the journey back across the Atlantic for a longer holiday, split between New York and Cape Cod. The first few days were spent in Manhattan, seeing the sights, before we took a plane operated by Trump Shuttle, the short-lived airline owned by the future US president, up to Martha's Vineyard, off the coast of Massachusetts.

Our transport turned out to be a small 12-seater plane, a prospect that thrilled me but terrified Chris. I enjoyed amazing views of the towering skyscrapers of the city as we climbed steeply after take-off from LaGuardia Airport, while a petrified Chris sat with her eyes locked on a game of Tetris on the Nintendo Game Boy I'd bought the day before at Macy's department store, just a few weeks after the console's US release.

Martha's Vineyard had long been renowned as the summer retreat of artists, musicians and politicians, with the Kennedy family arguably the most famous of them all. The cost of accommodation in summer would have been well out of our league, but we were travelling in October, well after the expensive holiday season had ended.

We arrived in the old whaling town of Edgartown, our home for the week, and found our hotel, a small quaint clapboard Victorian-era hotel frozen in time with a veranda and a white picket fence. The owner, a sweet old lady, served tea and sherry at four o'clock every day. In the late eighties and early nineties, many of Martha's Vineyard's towns were dry, a fact we only discovered when we arrived. Luckily, however, we had chosen a town that allowed the consumption of alcohol.

After we'd unpacked, we set off from the hotel to walk the short distance to the harbour. As we made our way down Main Street, flanked on either side by white wooden houses, I began to get an uneasy feeling that I had visited the town before. The impression grew the closer we got to the harbour.

As the town hall building came into view, a certainty gripped me. This was no trick of the mind. I knew this was definitely somewhere I had experienced before, but I'd never been to Cape Cod.

Amazingly, when I confided my bizarre secret to Chris, she confessed to having exactly the same feeling.

We walked past the shops and restaurants at the bottom of the street. As the area opened up to reveal the harbour, we were both stunned that it looked exactly as we had expected it to.

Still shocked by our otherworldly experiences, we made our way back to the hotel for the promised tea and sherry at four o'clock. The owner asked where we'd been and we told them we'd walked into town and down to the harbour, too embarrassed to reveal our uncanny tale.

"You know the Steven Spielberg film *Jaws* was filmed in Edgartown?" she asked.

Immediately it all made sense; our spooky deja vu was no more than a cinematic memory of a film classic we'd both seen numerous times.

The following day we hired bicycles, and after lunch we headed for the ferry to Chappaquiddick, the island just 500 feet from Edgartown and a few minutes on the ferry.

Chappy, as it's known to the locals, gained notoriety late

one night in 1969 when Senator Ted Kennedy, brother of the assassinated US president John F Kennedy, drove his car off a bridge on the island on his way back to the Edgartown ferry, killing his passenger, Mary Jo Kopechne. Kennedy left the scene of the accident and didn't report the crash to the police until 10 am the following morning. The incident is believed to have destroyed Kennedy's hopes of following his brother into the White House.

That afternoon, we decided to go in search of the infamous bridge. We peddled off the otherwise-empty ferry and on to a long thin headland that connected the landing strip to the rest of the island. Telephone poles flanked either side of the headland, and on the looping wires that hung between them sat a flock of crows. As we cycled along the headland, the birds followed us, perching on the hanging cables and moving from one loop to the other as we passed them. The unsettling sight of the birds following us, along with the constant squeaking made by one of the bikes as the pedals were turned, provided an eerie backdrop to our adventure.

We passed a deserted beach and beach huts and entered a wooded area where log cabins, reminiscent of those from *Friday the 13th* or countless other slasher horror movies, stood empty, the summer inhabitants having long since abandoned them.

Further and further we cycled into the woods, the wheel continuing to make its repetitive eerie squeak, echoing in the otherwise noiseless still air, and, as time wore on, the sun began to set, the shadows of the trees lengthening.

Suddenly we realised we were deep into the centre of the island and the light was dimming fast. We hadn't seen a living soul since we landed there, and the only sign of habitation we'd seen was a small wrecking yard with piles of rusting dismembered cars and trucks. We decided it was time to start pedalling in the other direction... and fast.

We reached the ferry with the light fast disappearing and admitted defeat in our quest to find the Mary Jo Kopechne bridge.

We cycled back up Main Street towards our hotel, locked our bikes up for the night and made our way through to the library room with its imposing fireplace, where we were unfortunately too late for tea and sherry. Hearing us entering, the kindly owner joined us and sat down to ask us about our day.

Learning where our bike journey had taken us, she leant in conspiratorially. "You know Chappaquiddick is where Ted Kennedy had his accident?"

We looked surprised and then nodded as if we'd only just made the connection.

"Do you know," she said, "there are people who go across on the ferry, just to see if they can see the bridge."

We both looked suitably shocked. "Really?" we said, shaking our heads. "How sick," we said in unison.

Shortly after the visit to *TV Guide* in the States, I had to travel to Germany with Murdoch Magazines' production director, Jasper Smith. The visit had two aims: the first was to discuss the German publisher Burda investing in the UK *TV Guide*, and the second was to see the publisher's German printing plant in Darmstadt.

I had no idea at the time that Sky's battle with its satellite competitor British Satellite Broadcasting (BSB) was draining Murdoch's News Corp organisation to such an extent that his ability to enter the TV listings market after deregulation was being put in jeopardy, hence the search to find a potential German partner.

I presented my plans for the magazine to Burda executives in Munich, as I had with the *TV Guide* team in Pennsylvania, and received a similar reaction. They thanked me for my presentation and placed copies of their

German TV magazines on the table, explaining why their editorial recipe was the perfect mix.

Their blueprint largely consisted of lots of photos and very little information about the TV programmes themselves. It had me puzzled as to why readers would buy a magazine that had less detail about the shows than they could get in their daily newspapers. I solved the mystery later that day when I bought a selection of German newspapers and discovered that their coverage of TV schedules was miniscule compared to the British tabloids, which often gave three or four pages to a day's TV.

From Munich, Jasper and I travelled on to Darmstadt to view the Burda printing plant in which Rupert Murdoch had bought a fifty per cent share and where it was hoped *TV Guide* would be printed using satellite technology to send the data from our London offices.

It was there that I was given a chilling message for Murdoch himself; one that when I later considered it, should have acted as a warning of what was in store for the Australian mogul and his business.

After the tour of the plant, we were taken to a restaurant in the town's Orangerie, a pretty baroque palace built around the start of the eighteenth century. Over a pleasant lunch, the boss of the print works explained that the town had sustained horrific bombing raids during World War Two. I told him that my own hometown, Clydebank, had suffered a similar experience.

We were getting on really well and when I expressed how much I was enjoying his choice of wine, a German Riesling from Baden, he bought me a couple of bottles to take home with me.

Then, suddenly, the mood changed. The smile disappeared from his face as he looked across the table at me, staring straight into my eyes. It was as if a switch had suddenly been thrown.

Slowly and quietly, he said, "We would like you to tell Mr Murdoch we want to see our half of the money."

It felt like I had suddenly been dropped into a scene from *The Godfather*. That I'd been given a message containing an unspoken threat to relay to my mafia boss. His change of character was chilling. It was obvious that the outstanding debt had been owed for a considerable amount of time and that Burda's patience was running out.

I assured him that I'd pass on the message. When Jasper and I discussed his request after lunch, however, we both decided that it was probably best not to attempt to communicate the message to Rupert via my boss and that, under the circumstances, we were best to simply forget the whole episode.

Within a few months, it became obvious that Rupert Murdoch's News Corp organisation was in serious trouble, having made a massive investment in satellite television and poured huge resources into the battle to win viewers.

When BSB had won a government licence to provide a satellite television service to the UK in 1986, it appeared to have been handed a complete monopoly. Murdoch had other ideas and announced that he was launching a rival direct-to-home service called Sky. What ensued was a vicious battle that drained Murdoch's coffers to an alarming degree, leading to the financial situation that brought about the demand for cash from the Burda printing plant executive.

Rumour has it, within the Murdoch organisation, that the business came within one afternoon of going bust that year. Whatever the truth, his financial plight was to have dramatic implications for my plans to launch *TV Guide* against *TV Times* and *Radio Times*.

The lobbying for the ending of the duopoly, helped greatly by Rupert Murdoch's close relationship with Prime Minister Margaret Thatcher, led to the expected deregulation of TV magazines in 1990. This allowed any publisher willing to pay a licence fee to produce a TV weekly that included BBC, ITV and Channel 4 listings for the first time.

The countdown was on but just as I was putting my plans into first gear, Murdoch's economic difficulties were to completely scupper them.

Just before Christmas 1990, expectations were high for *TV Guide*, which was enjoying rapidly growing sales. So it came as a bolt out of the blue when I was called into the managing director's office and told that the magazine would not be entering the market when deregulation took place the following March – and that from the next issue, *TV Guide* would become a monthly subscription-only magazine dedicated to Sky programmes and TV listings.

It appeared that Murdoch's banks had offered him a deal to keep his company afloat and back his satellite venture in exchange for an agreement that he would not develop any new projects until his finances were stable.

As we headed into the new year of 1991, I couldn't help but feel that my career had taken a sudden step backwards, as I prepared to edit a monthly version of *TV Guide* instead of entering the weekly battle against *TV Times* and *Radio Times* I'd long planned for. I had no idea that the new year would usher in a frightening new episode in my life and later another unexpected change of job.

# CHAPTER 12

For a number of months, I'd been lying in bed at night in Oxford and Cambridge Mansions contemplating my navel. Well, to be more exact, I'd been examining a small spot just six inches to the right of my belly button.

Over that space of time it appeared to have changed colour, a black speckle at the base of it slowly creeping up to invade more and more of the red blemish, which was itself smaller than the end of a cigarette.

Every few nights I'd express my unease about the progress of the encroaching dark patch to Chris and she'd reply, "If it's worrying you, go and see the doctor about it."

Finally, one night in late winter, I again raised the bed sheets to examine my wayward lesion, wafting cold air under the covers in the process.

Irritated, Chris snapped, "Either go and see the GP about it, or don't mention it ever again."

It had been obvious for some time that Chris, a trained theatre nurse, was concerned about the changing condition of the spot. She'd even gone as far as to recommend a surgeon, Chris Russell, for me to visit using the company's private health insurance once I had a referral from my GP.

Her reaction that night finally persuaded me to make an appointment. I visited our local doctor, walking the 10 minutes to the surgery at the far end of Paddington Street. After a short wait, my name was called and I entered her consulting room. Telling the locum doctor of my concerns, I lifted my shirt and showed her the spot, explaining that over the past few months one side of it had begun to turn black.

Pushing her glasses down her nose, she examined it. "And you would like this removed?" she asked curtly.

I said I would, and with a quick brusque nod of the head she began writing a letter.

"I'm sending you to St Mary's at Paddington to have the lesion frozen off," she informed me, sealing the envelope and handing it to me.

I mentioned the consultant Chris had recommended but she dismissed the idea, making me feel as if I was asking to see the Governor of the Bank of England to cash a cheque. The whole consultation was over in a matter of minutes.

I carried on to my office in Haymarket and called Chris to tell her the news.

She was furious. "You go back to the GP and you tell her you want to see Mr Russell," she ordered.

So, more frightened of Chris' reaction if I didn't follow her instructions than I was of a second encounter with the sour-faced doctor, I returned to Paddington Street that evening and demanded the referral.

Mr Russell was a charming gentle man, with a bedside manner my GP could have learnt a huge amount from. He examined the spot and concluded the appropriate course of action was to remove it and perform a biopsy.

I took the opportunity to ask him if he could also remove a small mole on my left hand between my thumb and my index finger. It was purely a cosmetic removal but it seemed sensible to have it seen to at the same time.

The procedure was a simple one, under local anaesthetic, and the following week Chris and I visited Mr Russell's consulting rooms in Harley Street to discover the results.

We were called into his office by his secretary. He was sitting behind a large wooden desk, and we took our seats opposite.

"Well," he started, "the good news is, the mole on your hand is absolutely fine."

I was immediately confused. He'd said, "the good news," which normally means there's bad news to follow, but I hadn't prepared myself for anything other than an all-clear prognosis.

"I'm afraid, the one on your stomach, however, is a malignant melanoma and I'd like to remove it as soon as possible." he continued.

Again, confusion reigned for me as I heard the words "malignant melanoma". Surely that's cancer, I thought, but he's just told me I've got it, so it can't be, can it?

As we left the office, Chris, as she generally is on such occasions, was controlled and measured in her response to my questions about the cancer, her medical training providing her with a greater insight as to what the diagnosis meant.

It wasn't until years later that I learned from a newspaper article that the mortality for malignant melanoma was extremely high in the early nineties. The worry wasn't the initial cancer but where it might have spread to in the body. Chris, on the other hand, was well aware of the prognosis.

Arrangements were made for the operation to take place at Fitzroy Hospital in Marylebone, where Mr Russell consulted and Chris was a theatre nurse. It was one of two private hospitals Chris worked in during that time, the other being the King Edward VII Hospital for Officers. King Edward VII was the Royal Family's favoured hospital, and Chris had nursed a number of them in her time there. Patient confidentiality meant that apart from acknowledging that she'd had a royal in the hospital, no other details were ever forthcoming, except for the information that one anonymous member of the family had been cared for after slicing her hand open making herself a jam sandwich!

Mr Russell had asked whether I would prefer a general or local anaesthetic for the operation at the Fitzroy and I'd plumped for local, assuming it would be a simpler option. The night before I was due to enter the hospital, however, I began to have second thoughts.

"Was I being very brave asking for a local," I asked Chris as we sat watching the evening's general election coverage, "because if I was, I really didn't mean to be."

She put my mind at rest, assuring me I wasn't. Later, however, she confessed that she had been slightly taken aback when I'd chosen not to be put under for the operation.

In theatre, Chris sat with me as Mr Russell operated and we chatted as he worked on removing the offending lesion. The operation was over very quickly, and the surgeon gave permission for me and Chris to head home.

Chris explained that wouldn't be possible, as her shift in theatre didn't finish for another couple of hours. Rather than have me wait at home in an empty flat, Mr Russell agreed it would be OK for me to have a drink in The Beehive and have Chris pick me up on the way past.

By the time Chris entered the pub that evening, I was on my third pint of Guinness, my shirt stretched over the top of my head to reveal the plaster that covered my wound, thoroughly enjoying the fact I'd chosen local rather than general anaesthetic.

The following week at a follow-up appointment with Mr Russell, he gave me the great news that all edges of the flesh he'd removed – six inches high, six inches wide and three inches deep – had proved negative for cancerous cells. He was fairly certain the cancer hadn't spread.

I thanked him again and, just as we were leaving, asked what would have happened if Chris hadn't given me the advice to see him.

"Well, it's quite simple," he assured me chillingly. "Within six to nine months, the cancer would have got to a major organ and would almost certainly have killed you."

He paused and then suggested, "I think you should take your wife out for a very special 'thank you' dinner tonight, don't you?"

It had been a dark and terrifying few weeks, but the feeling of rebirth after the all-clear offered me a new perspective on the world and I vowed never to take life for granted again.

Editing a monthly magazine targeted exclusively at Sky satellite viewers was far from where I had hoped my career would be that spring. As I was watching friends, colleagues and rivals producing innovative new magazines in the newly deregulated TV listings market, I was simply happy to be alive and married to a wonderful wife who had just helped save my life.

As spring gave way to summer, out of the blue I received a job offer that was to set my career back on course.

Early one June morning, as I sat at my desk in Murdoch Magazines' Haymarket offices, the phone rang. It was my old *TV Times* colleague Paul Parish, who had recently moved to *Radio Times*.

"Have you had a call from Terry Pavey yet?" he inquired.

Terry had been assistant editor at *TV Times* when I worked there and had been at the centre of the embarrassing events involving the complaints about the film *Another Country*. He was now the magazine's deputy editor.

"I haven't heard from Terry since I left *TV Times*," I told Paul. "Why would he be calling me?"

"Bridget Rowe's just been appointed editor of *The Sunday Mirror* and Terry's replacing her in the chair at *TV Times*," Paul revealed. "I think he'll struggle in that role and will need a deputy who can help him out. With your experience, you're the obvious choice."

I knew Paul held Terry in very poor regard, blaming him

for events that led to him leaving *TV Times*, but I didn't think for one minute that Terry would call me, particularly after the incident where he had ordered the letters of complaint should be pinned on the walls of the office.

Ten minutes later, my phone rang again. "Hello, Col," came a cocky voice I recognised. "How are you?" It was Terry and the conversation went exactly as Paul had predicted. We met later that evening at a pub north of Euston Road, on Terry's route home to Hertfordshire, and the deal was done within a day of the first phone call.

I was back at *TV Times* as deputy editor, but it was a very different set up from the one I'd left a few years before. Shortly after I joined Murdoch, the UK's biggest consumer publisher, IPC Magazines, known in the industry as the Ministry of Magazines, had bought the title from the group of TV companies who owned it. IPC had moved its offices to IPC headquarters, the 29-floor King's Reach Tower on London's South Bank, at the time the tallest building in England south of the Thames.

With the deregulation of the TV listings market having taken place in the spring of 1991, *TV Times* now had a large group of competitors. Others had entered the market in the way I had hoped to do with *TV Guide*, so IPC had launched a second TV title to tackle the new rivals – a cut-price magazine called *What's On TV*.

It was a completely different competitive landscape, but now that we were owned by a top-class publishing company, IPC, it offered huge and exciting opportunities.

Although it was a step down from the editor role I'd previously held, I enjoyed my new job as Terry's deputy. I was a smaller fish but in a much larger pond, as *TV Times* was still the second best-selling magazine in Britain.

The cancer scare had also changed my mindset. I decided that Mark Twain's advice – "Twenty years from now you will be more disappointed by the things you didn't do than by the things you did" – held a great deal of water.

I was also haunted by the memory of a former colleague I'd worked with during my first spell at *TV Times*. Planning for retirement in a number of years, he'd bought a beautiful large property in Norfolk, too far from London to commute daily, and had spent four nights a week living in a rented room in the capital. He returned home on a Thursday night and travelled back to London on Sunday evenings.

It meant he only saw his wife and young family three days a week, but he believed that his sacrifice was offset by the future happiness they would all share when he took early retirement and could settle down in their idyllic home. Tragically, a short time before he was due to retire, his wife died of cancer and his cherished plans were destroyed.

"Live for today" became my motto. So when a reader's offer for a voyage from New York to Southampton on the *Queen Elizabeth 2* arrived on my desk one morning, I decided to go for it. I dived next door to the office of the marketing manager, Matt Preston, and asked him if he could get me a staff deal on the already attractive offer.

A tall, portly figure, with a great sense of humour, Matt organised an upgrade for me and Chris that saw us enjoying a much more luxurious experience than we would have otherwise been able to afford.

Matt emigrated to Australia a couple of years later and eventually made his name as co-host and judge on *MasterChef Australia*, leading to book deals and his own weekly food column syndicated across a series of newspapers Down Under. Such was the success of Matt's incumbency as host of *Masterchef Australia* that in 2010 the one and only election debate between prime ministerial candidates Julia Gillard and Tony Abbott was forced to move as it clashed with the final of the competition.

Being Clydebank-built, a journey on the *QE2* obviously had a personal appeal to me. I'd watched from my parents' house high above the town as the ship slowly began to appear above the buildings, eventually dwarfing them, and I remember the excitement as the funnel was finally lifted into place.

As a member of the burgh council, Dad had been invited to attend a tour of the finished ship, and he and Mum had taken a seven-year-old me along that afternoon. I even have a photo of me smiling at the camera with my hands reaching up to grab the steering wheel.

My pride as we set off from New York harbour, brass bands playing in the background as we passed the Statue of Liberty, knew no bounds. My only regret is that we didn't spend the extra money to take the since-retired Concorde on the first leg of the journey, from London to New York. A few years later, during my son Alexander's early years, it was to become a regular visitor as it flew over our garden in Surrey, and we would rush out to watch it streak past.

I'd worried that five days at sea might drag but the journey whizzed by with much of our time taken up simply people-watching. As a journalist on board, I was invited with Chris to a drinks party in the captain's cabin. As we entered his room with the evening's other guests, the captain pointed to a photo of the launching of the ship on the wall and asked the collected guests if they knew where it had been taken.

"It's John Brown's Shipyard in Clydebank and the month is September 1967," I piped up from the back of the crowd.

The captain was amazed at my knowledge until I explained my background and the bond I felt with the ship. It turned out that he had been the captain of the *QE2* during its construction, had lived in Clydebank in the months prior to the launch and knew many of my father's former council colleagues. In the end, we spent much of the drinks party swapping stories about the town.

205

The voyage ended in Southampton early on the final morning. Faced with the prospect of a train journey back to London Waterloo and the underground home from there, we decided to have one last taste of luxury and hopped in a taxi back to Marylebone. After my earlier brush with skin cancer, life we agreed was for living!

With the new all-channel TV guides, including *TV Times* and publisher IPC's own new launch *What's On TV*, selling in huge numbers, IPC decided it was time to look at launching a third TV magazine. The boom in TV titles coincided with a huge increase in the number of viewers subscribing to Murdoch's Sky satellite TV, so a title focussing on that emerging platform seemed to make sense and we recruited several research panels to assess the opportunity.

On the first night of research, we observed the participants sitting behind a one-way mirror, transparent glass on our side and a normal mirror on the respondents' side, as Linda Jones, a researcher I would eventually work with for more than thirty years, quizzed them about their use of TV.

At the time, coverage of channels other than BBC, ITV and Channel 4 was sparse in mass market newspapers and weekly magazines, and viewers who wanted listings information about satellite channels bought one of three monthly magazines that contained four weeks schedules but scant detail.

I was excited by the prospect of launching a new magazine and was certain that the idea of a weekly title offering the same amount of space to satellite TV as was enjoyed by the traditional channels would appeal to readers.

For nearly an hour and a half, it appeared I was wrong. The more Linda dangled the prospect of an exciting new magazine in front of the research group, the more they appeared to be entrenched in their current pattern of buying a weekly magazine for the terrestrial channels and a monthly for satellite.

Things were looking very negative when just before the end of the session, Linda popped out of the research and into our room to check if we had any further questions. I'd worked on some innovative page designs for what I hoped would be the second round of research. They were very rough, but I realised the project was probably dead in the water unless we could get some positivity out of these research groups.

I thrust the printed pages into Linda's hands and asked her to get the group's opinion, stressing that they were very early ideas.

Slowly but surely the group began to become more enthusiastic about the proposition, and before the end of the group it began to feel as if there might just be an opportunity in the market.

Linda introduced the pages much earlier in the evening's second session and the interest in the potential magazine increased still further. By the end of group two, we began to believe we were onto something.

The initial problem wasn't that the first group didn't want the magazine, they just couldn't conceive what it might give them that they didn't already have. It was only when we offered them examples of the various new elements it might contain that they could visualise a need for it. That evening, I learnt an important lesson that often a dummy version can help explain an abstract idea much better than words. It was a principle that was to later help me greatly when developing projects in the digital realm.

More research groups followed, and the magazine grew from an idea to a concept to a full-blown dummy issue, which was well received in wider research. We knew sport and movies were two of the main drivers for satellite TV, so we focussed on developing tools that would help readers easily find the events and films they wanted.

Strangely, another major success was the addition of German channel listings. At the time, Sky offered nothing like the number of channels that are now available, and viewers often found themselves still unhappy with the choice. On those occasions they would flick through the foreign channels, predominantly German, that could also be accessed through their set-top box as they beamed their signals from the same Astra satellite as Sky.

While most of our readers couldn't speak a foreign language, they could still enjoy sport and music programmes without having to worry about translations. The same, of course, could be said for the late-night porn films that were a staple of the German offerings.

A concise two-page section at the back of the magazine offered enough information about the schedules for viewers to plan their evening's Teutonic treats and gave us another unique selling point.

Months of research eventually led to the launch of the magazine in spring 1993. There was much discussion as to what the title should be before *TV & Satellite Week* was agreed on, and the first issue finally hit the shelves with Arnold Schwarzenegger on the cover.

Sales, however, failed to come anywhere near the target and after four or five weeks it looked as if the magazine might not survive the summer as it was losing tens of thousands of pounds every week.

My publishing director, Linda Lancaster-Gaye, called me into her office for a crisis meeting. We sat on the floor around a small coffee table in the centre of her office as she laid out all the options that could affect profitability.

We were already running on a small staff, so cutting headcount wasn't an option. We agreed to cut paper quality, print the cover on thinner paper and reduce the number of pages, while also increasing the magazine's price. It felt like a recipe for disaster but, faced with ballooning losses, it was our only option.

The following week, we saw a tiny upward blip in the sales chart, followed the next week by another marginal increase and, as the weeks turned to months, circulation began to climb.

By the end of the first year, the magazine sales were up more than 25 per cent year-on-year and it led to my second British Society of Magazine Editors Awards nomination. I once again failed to win the award, but this time at least I saved myself the embarrassment of premature celebration.


The spring of 1993 also brought the wonderful news that we were going to have a baby. It was something early in our relationship that Chris and I had agreed we wanted but it wasn't until a false alarm the previous year that we decided it was time to try.

During a visit to friends in Coventry, we'd both been shocked when Chris realised she might be pregnant. Our first reaction was one of horror as we didn't feel ready for such a major event. But by the time we'd bought a test kit and Chris confirmed she wasn't having a baby, the idea had become firmly lodged in our minds and we decided that we were ready for parenthood.

Throughout the pregnancy, the baby was known as Pugs, after a World War Two advisor to Winston Churchill, Hastings "Pug" Ismay, whose picture we'd seen during a Cabinet War Rooms tour in Westminster soon after we discovered Chris was pregnant.

A few months into the pregnancy, I was approached by a headhunter and offered the role of deputy editor of Reader's Digest Books for Australasia, a role I was told would lead to me taking over as editor of the organisation within a year, when the current incumbent retired. Chris and I considered the pros and cons of the offer carefully before deciding that a new job, a new area of expertise, a new country and a new baby were just too many life changes at one time. It's a decision we've never regretted.

In December 1993, Pugs was born at St Mary's Paddington and immediately named after my dad, Alexander. We were now a happy little family of three.

# CHAPTER 13

As *TV & Satellite Week*'s sales continued in a very satisfyingly upward trajectory, I had nothing but positive news to report during the annual business review I presented to the company's board. The magazine's success meant I had few plans to report regarding editorial enhancements. Instead, I turned to an area that had fired my imagination since my visits to *TV Guide* in Pennsylvania – the future of publishing.

Tim Berners-Lee had only invented the World Wide Web a handful of years before. Up until 1993, it was largely the domain of academia, with the first public browser not available until late 1991, but I could see that it was about to change the world.

When I visited it, *TV Guide* in the States was beginning to offer digital content to readers through online internet services such as Compuserve and America Online (later renamed AOL), walled gardens that provided World Wide Web-style content via proprietary software using dial-up phone modems. They were also exploring the possibility of providing content for electronic programme guides (EPGs) on TVs.

The opportunities offered by this emerging technology excited me greatly, but I also saw the threats that it might pose for magazines in general.

I'd been fascinated by technology since my brother Ian brought a very early electronic calculator home for me from a holiday in Tenerife in the early seventies. It could only add, subtract and divide but I was smitten with it. In the early eighties, I bought a Sinclair home computer, which saved and loaded data from audio cassettes, and later that decade an Amstrad word processor and then an early Apple computer. When the Apple Newton, one of the earliest personal digital assistants, was released in 1993, I ordered one from the States at great cost. I just had to have the latest gadget.

I spent the first half of that year's board presentation discussing the successful launch of *TV & Satellite Week*, and the second half outlining the threats and opportunities that the coming digital world would bring.

It's amazing to think that the internet and the World Wide Web were hardly known about in the UK at the time, and most of what I had to say was totally new to the IPC board. Sticking with my belief that it's better to demonstrate a concept than to ask an audience to imagine it, I mocked up a Powerpoint slideshow that, when I clicked buttons in a certain order, gave the impression of an interactive TV service, much like Sky now offers.

I included a home shopping service linked to video recipes too, explaining that one day customers would be able to read our magazines' recipes on screen and order the ingredients and other groceries to be delivered to their home.

The presentation proved a hit and later that day I was seconded from my editorship to become "multimedia development manager" for the company, entrusted with learning more about the effects digital would have on publishing and seeking out opportunities to partner with other companies.

I became a digital evangelist for the company, attending conferences to gather knowledge and speaking at others, both internally and externally, to spread the word about the coming digital revolution and IPC's plans for it.

I gave my board presentation to the whole company at an event in the National Film Theatre on London's South Bank and to a wider audience of senior executives from IPC's parent company Reed Elsevier. At the latter event, when I showed the Powerpoint mock-up of my home shopping application, the concept raised a ripple of laughter from a small percentage of the room. Yet, just over three years later Tesco began to experiment with their own online shopping service. The world was changing very rapidly.

I began to build a network of contacts in other industries that were starting to investigate digital products, and soon I had the sign-off from our corporate bosses at Reed for major investments in two exciting projects. The first involved interactive TV and the second involved CD-ROM technology.

I learnt that BT was planning an experimental interactive TV service in Colchester and negotiated a deal whereby IPC would exclusively produce a series of on-screen magazines for the service. The concept involved viewers selecting a magazine brand and then accessing text, photo and video articles to be displayed on their TV screen.

The trial consisted of 150 content providers, from Hollywood film studies to UK charities, offering everything from shopping to entertainment, banking to education, providing an on-screen service across normal BT telephone lines in a way that the internet couldn't conceive of doing at the time. Rudimentary software to provide streaming video didn't appear for the World Wide Web until 1995.

For me, the most important aspect of the trial was to experiment with an electronic version of our TV magazines, as it appeared obvious to me that an on-screen electronic programme guide would offer a major threat to *TV Times* and *What's On TV*.

BT, however, was more interested in the other magazine titles we were bringing to the party. Its enthusiasm for *Hair* magazine-style guides, *Golf Monthly* playing tips and *Woman and Home* beauty advice was noticeably greater than its interest in a listings title.

In the end, the partnership was dissolved because a TV guide prototype was too far down BT's list of priorities.

Soon afterwards, however, a Cambridge company called Online Media announced it was developing a similar trial in its local cable franchise area, and the cable infrastructure, which was already designed to carry video, offered much more bandwidth to experiment with. I met with its team and we agreed to produce *TV Times on Screen* for the Cambridge project.

The trial also involved working with a small group of major partners, including ITN, the Post Office, Anglia Television, Nat West Bank, the BBC and Tesco, ironically offering home shopping through the TV much as I'd predicted a few years earlier.

We worked with the software engineers at Online Media to produce the UK's first electronic programme guide, some time before Sky's own digital on-screen listings guide saw the light of day, an achievement that was to offer IPC a solid commercial opportunity.

The growth of the UK cable industry, made up of a plethora of small companies each with their own geographical franchise areas, was stalling as Rupert Murdoch's Sky satellite service continued to grow. The prospect of a next-generation digital Sky service, offering many more channels and much more interactivity, was a frightening prospect looming on the horizon.

A decision was taken that cable had to offer one consistent digital service across all the companies if it was to have any hope of competing against Sky. Derek Lewis, a senior TV executive, was chosen to chair the project, which was christened New Horizons.

Following our success in Cambridge, Lewis approached IPC about developing an electronic programme guide that would sit at the heart of the service. The deal involved IPC investing money in the project, but with its parent company Reed Elsevier fast becoming the leading digital player in business-to-business publishing, and aware of the threat digital posed to our highly profitable print publications, the opportunity was quickly embraced.

The other two partners in the deal were Flextech, which owned several cable and satellite TV channels including *UK Gold*, and Telewest, one of the larger cable franchisees. My opposite number at Flextech was Ashley Highfield, who later moved to the BBC where, as Director of Future Media and Technology, he was responsible for the development of the BBC iPlayer.

Working with an interactive design agency, Mousepower, we developed the guide to a prototype stage when disaster struck. Reed Elsevier decided that it wanted to concentrate on business publishing and put IPC Magazines up for sale, resulting in further investment in the cable project being stopped.

In order to ensure the project hit its strict deadline, the original agreement between IPC and the cable industry stipulated that should there be any interruption to funding by any of the parties, the work developed up until that point would be owned by the other partners. As a result, we were forced to hand over our rights to the prototype. The group continued their work, and when a UK-wide digital cable service was launched, the on-screen guide was largely the one we developed with Mousepower.

A footnote to the project involves an infamous interview involving former British Home Secretary Michael Howard. Following his earlier successes in industry, in 1993, four years before his involvement with the cable project, Derek Lewis had been appointed Director General of Her Majesty's Prisons, part of a Conservative government initiative to bring successful business leaders into public service roles.

Prior to the release of a damning report into prisoner escapes, Howard had taken the opportunity to blame the prison service for the scandal, in an interview with Jeremy

Paxman on BBC's *Newsnight*. When asked whether he had threatened to overrule Lewis when he sacked a prison governor, Howard failed on numerous occasions to give a direct answer. The interview turned into a pantomime as Paxman eventually asked the same question, "Did you threaten to overrule him?" fourteen times.

The interview took place the night before one of our regular New Horizon meetings and as Lewis entered the room, we all asked, as one, "Did he threaten to overrule you?" A huge smile broke out across the former TV executive's face, but we ended the meeting none the wiser as to the answer. The interview was no laughing matter for Howard, however, as many believe it contributed to the failure of his bid for the Conservative leadership that same year.

The second of the major digital projects given the go-ahead was the world's first magazine on CD-ROM, the storage discs similar to audio CDs that held all kinds of data including video. To be truthful, it was not just the first but also nearly the last publication of its kind.

At the time, in the mid-nineties, a number of magazines were publishing promotional CD-ROM discs on their covers, offering video game demos or free computer software. But it struck me that the audio and video capabilities created by home computers offered journalists the opportunity to tell stories in an exciting innovative new way that wasn't being exploited.

Co-incidentally a small start-up called Zone UK arrived at my office one day with a fully thought-out product that fitted perfectly with my idea. They proposed publishing a magazine solely on CD-ROM featuring a selection of IPC magazine brands that contained video, audio and graphics of the quality normally seen in top-of-the-range computer games.

The cost of the project was eye-watering and involved IPC investing a six-figure sum. However, I managed to sell the idea to the board and we began to develop the magazine using content and branding from three titles – the prestigious music weekly *New Musical Express* (*NME*), its now-defunct monthly sister-magazine *Vox* and the respected science and technology weekly *New Scientist* – as well as content developed by Zone UK.

Deals were struck with major retailers, from newsagents such as WHSmith to music and games stores such as Virgin Megastore and HMV, and the price was fixed at £15.99.

Called *UnZip*, the disc provided six hours of entertainment with an internet primer from *New Scientist*, a multimedia profile of the group Bomb the Bass from *NME* and *Vox* reviews and previews of music, films and computer games. Zone UK provided a look at Manga, an interactive cartoon, and a feature on street art.

Rather than signpost things too heavily, we opted for a design that encouraged a process of discovery – for instance, dragging a character's ear up or down increased or decreased the volume.

The finished disc was a triumph, and the trade press gave it rave reviews, with *Publishing* magazine describing it as "pushing back the frontiers of UK multimedia publishing" and "a hard act for other UK publishers to follow".

We produced more than 100,000 discs. Financially, the product was... a complete and utter failure, with just a few thousand sold nationwide.

Whether the concept was too difficult to understand, the price was too high, the process of discovery too complicated or a mix of all three, the British public rejected it completely.

We were deflated, and my stock at IPC undoubtedly fell quite considerably. We now had a huge hole in the budget and more than 90,000 CD-ROM discs in storage.

Such had been the critical acclaim that had met the

magazine's launch, however, that I thought it worthwhile entering it for the Milia d'Or Awards at the Cannes New Media Festival the following spring. I'd attended the previous year's event and planned to make the trip again, tagging on a few days holiday with Chris and Alexander.

To my surprise, we were one of the three titles shortlisted. As the date of the awards grew closer, I had an idea. Could we dispose of the overabundant copies of *UnZip* at the festival, and simultaneously raise the profile of the company as a digital publisher?

So, while Chris, Alexander and I were flying to Nice Airport, another member of the team, Nick, was driving from London to the south of France in a huge van stuffed full of the unsold copies of the disc.

The CD-ROM came in a box the size of a DVD case, and Nick began distributing these to delegates from around the world on the Promenade de la Croisette the day before the festival began. They were eagerly received, but immediately the boxes were discarded and the discs pocketed, leaving a sea of *UnZip* packaging washing down the promenade for as far as the eye could see every day of the festival. Unintentionally, we had created a viral advertising campaign for the unknown brand.

The night of the awards arrived, and I donned my tuxedo and headed to the Palais des Festivals for the ceremony. *UnZip*'s rivals for the award were *The Microsoft Wine Guide* and a disc tracing the journey along America's famous Route 66. It seemed certain the excellent encyclopaedia from the software giant, with its slick videos featuring wine expert and TV presenter Oz Clarke, would win, but I wasn't going to let that upset my evening.

I bumped into a lawyer from the company we'd used to draw up the contract for the interactive TV trials and we sat together as the ceremony began. As each of the nominees was announced, a short film of the disc's contents was beamed onto the huge theatre screen before the presenter announced the winning entry.

As he began to read "And the winner is…", I tensed as I waited for the name "*The Microsoft Wine Guide*". But after a tension-building pause, I was totally shocked when he announced "*UnZip*". Applause filled the packed theatre, adding to the disorientation I was experiencing as I sat rooted to my seat.

"Go on," my lawyer companion encouraged me, patting me on the shoulder and pointing towards the stage.

I made my way along the row, bumping knee after knee as I went, until I reached the aisle, up onto the stage. The applause continued in the background and the video of *UnZip* played once again on the screen.

As the clapping died down, I found myself standing next to French composer Jean-Michel Jarre, whose ground-breaking album *Oxygéne* I had loved in the mid-seventies. Jarre looked across at me and began to pay tribute to the disc the team and I had created. As he smiled and gesticulated, it was a surreal moment watching this hero from my teenage years.

The occasion took a terrifying twist for me moments later, however, when he gestured towards the podium for me to reply. His eulogy had been delivered entirely in French, my grasp of which was proficient enough to order a wide variety of alcoholic drinks but not to follow Jean-Michel's fast-moving tribute.

I grabbed the podium tightly and thanked everyone I could think of, in the manner of an Oscar winner, before returning to my seat with the winged statue trophy.

Whether the unintentional marketing campaign that saw us plaster the streets of Cannes with *UnZip* boxes had any effect on the final outcome of the awards competition, we'll never know. But one thing's for sure – the refuse collectors in the French city would not have handed us any awards after that weekend.

Despite the competition success and the resultant praise the team and I received, I continued to regard *UnZip* as an unmitigated failure, having invested more than £100,000 in the launch and returned pitiful sales.

Sitting with Alun Anderson, the editor of *New Scientist*, at an awards ceremony one night a couple of years later, we were reminiscing about the fun we'd had developing the disc with his team. I described the project as a cul-de-sac in our digital development.

Alun was taken aback by my verdict on the project. He'd launched the *New Scientist* website, *Planet Science*, one of the few early magazine sites to make a profit, some months after the launch of *UnZip*. "The work my team did on the CD-ROM cut our website development time by months, taught the team important lessons about interactivity and allowed us to beat competitor sites to market," he enthused.

Although CD-ROM wasn't a publishing platform suited for magazines, what the disc did give us, and later some other pioneering publishers, was the ability to experiment with audio and video content before the internet could offer the capability, positioning us firmly ahead of the game.

The development work on *UnZip* was an important part of the company's journey to a digital publishing future and pushed it further up the learning curve than any of its competitors. Taken as a long-term investment, rather than a short-term project launch, it was money very well spent.

Further proof of the influence *UnZip* had on the industry came when I was invited to Luxembourg to speak at a European Commission conference discussing the future of electronic publishing. A delegate approached me during the lunch break and asked if I had been part of the development of the CD-ROM magazine. I told him I had, and he revealed that he'd received the free copy of *UnZip* at the Cannes Milia d'Or festival and it had inspired him to create his company, which had become one of the leading digital publishers in Scandinavia.

By 1996, IPC Magazines was building a name for itself as an early investor in digital publishing. As publisher of *New Scientist*, a colleague Jonathan Newby had launched the magazine's website, *Planet Science*, and a second site for *New Musical Express*, *NME.com*, had also been created. Jonathan and I had become IPC's digital face: Jonathan looking after the publishing aspects of development, while I took care of editorial.

We were approached in the summer of that year by an organisation called Index Vanguard. It was an advanced technology research group for senior-level executives, headquartered in Santa Monica, California, meeting six times a year in locations around the world to explore how digital technology was going to change the world.

Jonathan and I were invited to lunch at a house on one of the squares in London's upmarket Fitzrovia, where the company wined and dined us before the invitation to join was offered. The promise of access to many of the most influential visionaries of the emerging digital age was enormous, but so was the eye-watering sum we were being asked to pay for membership of the group.

They offered us the opportunity to sample one of the conferences in London in September. Unfortunately, Jonathan couldn't attend but I enthusiastically accepted the invitation.

Arriving at the Royal Garden Hotel in Kensington, I registered and made my way into the main hall where the first face I saw, talking to other delegates, was Nicholas Negroponte. A professor at the prestigious Massachusetts Institute of Technology, Negroponte was a visionary who had just written *Being Digital*, predicting how digital technology would shape the world's future. I was a huge fan

221

and was awed to see him across the room.

The conference offered an amazing insight into how dramatically digital technology was about to change our lives, and was attended by blue chip companies from the UK and across the globe – British Airways, AT&T, BP, Glaxo Wellcome, Marks & Spencer, CNN, BT, Merrill Lynch, DuPont...

I was immediately sold on joining but when I returned to the office Jonathan was more reluctant. Eventually, I convinced him that the money was an important investment, and we approached the board and were given the go ahead. We agreed to each attend alternate conferences but that we would both go to Pasadena, California, for the first in November.

The same impressive line-up of names that graced the London conference attended the Californian event. As well as Negroponte, the speakers included C Gordon Bell, one of the world's leading authorities on computer design and architecture who designed the innovative VAX computer system in the eighties, Alan Kay, who at Xerox and Apple invented the file and folder interface that made home computers accessible to millions, and Peter Cochrane, head of the advance research department at British Telecom.

I was very keen that Jonathan was impressed by the event, as I had had to work so hard persuading him to invest the money, but unfortunately the conference got off to a bad start.

After the initial session, we were all packed onto a coach for an interminable journey through crawling LA traffic to Alan Kay's home, where we were promised "a treat". Jonathan was far from amused by the wasted time spent transporting us from the conference venue in Pasadena to the house in Santa Monica.

As the coach turned into Alan's street, I looked up at the road sign hanging from a street light and saw "Rockingham

Avenue". That rang a bell, I thought, but before I could work out why, someone else in the coach shouted, "Are we going to visit OJ?"

Rockingham Drive was the home that OJ Simpson's Bronco was heading for when it was chased along the Californian highway by police following the murder of his ex-wife Nicole Brown.

Stopping outside Alan's home in the upmarket area of Brentwood, we headed into a huge barn-sized building next to his sizable house. We climbed polished oak stairs up to a balcony overlooking an enormous hall, set out with row after row of pews. Taking our seats in matching polished oak benches in the upper floor and looking down, a huge baroque church organ dominated our view of the wall in front.

Once all the conference delegates were seated, Alan Kay walked proudly out of the shadows, towards the bench positioned in front of the organ. Positioning his hands carefully on the keys, he played the booming opening notes of the *Phantom of the Opera* theme – Daaaa, da da da da da! Then he turned with a flourish and a beaming smile towards the seated delegates, who gave him a rousing round of applause.

"Jesus," I heard Jonathan whisper under his breath.

It was obvious that Alan's keyboard mastery was not impressing him, and I imagine he thought I'd lost my senses subscribing to such a fiasco. The subsequent lecture about the seventeenth-century Northern German Baroque organ Alan had installed in his home had me questioning my judgement too.

Alan next introduced Kevin Kelly, founding editor of *Wired* magazine, whose first words were, "The trouble with American TV is we don't make enough bad programmes."

This elicited a hushed, "Good grief," from Jonathan, as he thrust his head into his hands.

223

Soon after, however, things began to change. What Kelly was getting at was that TV wasn't taking chances, and to be safe was producing a string of lacklustre shows. In order to create ground-breaking TV, you need to take risks that would inevitably lead to some stinkers. You can't make an omelette without breaking eggs. That was, he observed, a hugely important lesson as we entered the new digital age.

Jonathan agreed with his conclusion and, as the conference proceeded, his misgivings about it began to diminish.

The following day, we received a mind-blowing demonstration of a device that, at the time, appeared to be straight out of a science fiction movie. In a session called *The Future of Print*, Joseph Jacobson, a professor at MIT Media Labs, demonstrated something he called a microencapsulated electrophoretic display or electronic ink.

It was a display device that mimicked the look of ordinary ink on paper and on which entire books could be downloaded. What we were looking at was a very early prototype of the Amazon Kindle, which uncannily launched exactly 11 years later on 19 November 2007. It was a fascinating sneak peek into the future, and one of many the conferences were to deliver over the coming year.


The pioneering digital work Jonathan and I were doing, along with the resultant conference speeches and articles in trade journals, led to a number of job offers from headhunters for both of us. When IPC Magazines were sold by Reed Elsevier to Cinven, a private equity company, Jonathan left the company to join Reed as managing director of a group of scientific magazines, leaving me to take over as both editor-in-chief and publishing director for the new media division.

Events could have taken a very different course a couple of years earlier, however, when my experience in digital publishing almost resulted in me forming an unexpected business partnership with a TV action hero.

As I said earlier, I first met Gareth Hunt at Stringfellow's nightclub in the early eighties and, at the time, he came across as arrogant and egotistical. By the time I met him again, when The Krankies starred with him in *Aladdin* at the Civic Theatre in Darlington in 1993, he had changed beyond recognition.

Now in his early 50s and happily settled in Surrey with his third wife, Amanda, and a young son, he had lost the air of self-importance that I'd experienced when we'd first met, at a time when his face was a regular on British TV screens.

Gareth first made his name as footman Frederick Norton in the seventies series *Upstairs, Downstairs* before gaining worldwide fame as secret agent Mike Gambit, alongside Joanna Lumley and Patrick McNee, in *The New Avengers*.

A few years later, he famously gave birth to a national gesture called the "Nescafe handshake", which the *Urban Dictionary* website explains, "originates from a TV coffee advert of the 70s/80s starring Gareth Hunt. He holds several coffee beans in a half-clenched fist then shakes them in a way reminiscent of a hand job. The relationship with Gareth Hunt is further strengthened since he was considered to be a bit of a wanker."

That may have been the case in the early eighties, but the Gareth Hunt I met in Darlington was a changed individual. Delightful, charming and funny, he was terrific company and we shared a fascination with new technology.

One night in the bar after the pantomime, Gareth and I got into a long conversation about the possibility of producing a digital version of *Spotlight*, the set of books used to cast most UK theatre, TV and film productions.

Since 1927, the publishers had charged annual fees from actors and actresses to display a photo, personal details and agent contact details in the book's pages. Gareth could see the opportunity to create a digital version and began discussing producing a set of CD-ROMs that would include not just photos but also videos of actors performing.

I shared Gareth's enthusiasm about the potential that such a project could offer, but convinced him that an online platform would be far more flexible and scalable than CD-ROM and assured him the technology required was just around the corner.

We agreed to develop the idea further and met several times after the pantomime ended to shape the concept. Gareth began to gather financial backing and pledges of support from a variety of fellow actors, including his *New Avengers* co-star Joanna Lumley. The project began to take shape in our minds.

Unfortunately, at this stage, Gareth introduced another partner to the enterprise. Discussing what would happen if the project hit financial problems once we had begun collecting fees from subscribers, he declared that he would have no scruples about holding on to the money that had been already invested. It was a deal breaker for me, and I bowed out of the venture at that point, wishing Gareth luck.

The development work never did come to fruition. Many years later, *Spotlight* produced its own digital online version, which now successfully sits alongside the nearly century-old print edition.

As the digital side of IPC expanded with the launch of numerous websites and other projects, the company changed its name from IPC Magazines to IPC Media, and I found my role as publishing director taking me further and further away from the creative side of the business that I loved. So when the managing director of the TV titles, Sly Bailey, asked me to return to her group as executive editor in charge of new launches, I jumped at the chance.

My remit was to extend the reach of our TV listings

magazines from print into as many digital platforms as I could. We decided, however, that instead of using one of the existing titles – *TV Times*, *What's On TV* or *TV & Satellite Week* – there should be a new brand, *Unmissable TV*.

Digital publishing was now a major part of IPC's operations. As our private equity owners Cinven sought to sell the company, the spotlight was very much on developing that aspect of the business.

So, when a royal visitor was due to visit the company's King's Reach Tower headquarters in London, it was no surprise that my team and I were lined up to meet them.

Activity at King's Reach began long before I became aware we were to have a VIP guest, with the smell of fresh paint filling the stairwells of the 29-floor building for weeks before the announcement that King Charles, then Prince Charles, was to tour the offices.

IPC was the UK's biggest publisher, producing more than 100 weekly and monthly magazines and a growing number of websites, and my role was to introduce the Prince of Wales to the digital side of the business.

Charles was being hailed in the media as a modern progressive royal. Much was being made of the fact that he regularly conversed with Prince William, who at the time was enjoying a gap year in the wilds of Patagonia, by email, still a relatively new means of communication for many in the UK. I suspected, therefore, that he would be fascinated by some of the developments we were working on.

The day before the appointed date, and again early on the day of the royal visit, the royal protection unit and their sniffer dogs were led through our floor of the building, investigating every nook and cranny of the office.

I hadn't written any kind of speech, preferring to busk it to make the occasion as spontaneous as possible. When my managing director, Caroline, appeared with Charles and ushered him towards me, I knew exactly the areas I wanted to demonstrate to him.

After a bit of small talk, I launched into an explanation of how we had created *Unmissable TV* as a website and had plans to launch it on PDAs, palm-held computers that functioned as personal organisers but also provided email and internet access, WAP, the early internet-connected phones, and interactive TV.

Feeling pretty happy with my short but succinct explanation of our innovative strategy and the technologies we planned to harness to fulfil our plans, I looked up from the computer screen to see a rather bemused look on the face of the royal guest.

Then a smile returned to Charles' face as he gently patted a pile of *TV Times* print magazines and declared, "As long as you still keep producing these, I'll be happy."

It seemed the future monarch, hailed in the British press as the very essence of a twenty-first century techno prince, was having a little trouble with the ideas and concepts I was introducing to him.

The tour hadn't gone quite how I'd expected, but I'd held back the most impressive demonstration until last. Over the years, *TV Times* had compiled a vast collection of film reviews, first on cards in huge filing cabinets and latterly on a computer database. Although smaller in size, it was like the Internet Movie Database (IMDB), which had recently been bought by Amazon founder Jeff Bezos – fully searchable by film title, genre, actor, director, you name it. We were very proud of it and I planned to end Prince Charles' visit by displaying its ability.

"Every major film that's been made is on the database," I enthusiastically told him. "Just pick a film title."

Charles thought for a few seconds, staring at the computer monitor and fiddling with his cufflinks, and finally mumbled, "Eh… What about *Casablanca*?"

I nodded and gestured for him to take the seat in front of

the screen. Looking slightly perplexed, he sat down. Staring at the keyboard for a long moment, he hit the letter C. Then, after another long pause, the letter A. Agonisingly slowly, one by one, he hunted for the correct letters and pecked at the keyboard. With the title finally complete, I gestured for him to hit the Return key and the film's details flashed up on the display.

"Marvellous," he agreed, as I leant over to assist him with the next keyboard search.

I can only conclude that if the Prince of Wales did regularly email Prince William, as was so heavily hyped in the media, it must have taken up a great deal of the future king's busy schedule.


Coincidentally, one of King Charles' favourite magazines is *Country Life*, which many years later my friend and fellow editor Mark Hedges managed to persuade His Majesty to edit on a number of occasions. Back around the time of Charles' visit, I was delighted to be asked by the then editor, Clive Aslet, to contribute my thoughts on how technology would shape the twenty-first century for the magazine's Millennium issue, published in December 1999, that looked back over 20 centuries of the British Isles and forward to the future.

In his article, looking towards the coming century, Clive quoted me as saying that we "...would soon receive information – pre-selected for our own preferences – on objects as humble as fridge magnets. As we take out our milk for our cereal, we can glance at the fridge door to check the news headlines and top TV viewing recommendations, prioritised according to the subjects that we are interested in.

"Similar information will be available on petrol pumps: after all, in our increasingly busy lives, who wants to stand at a pump for three precious minutes, simply putting petrol into a tank? By the end of five years, information will be everywhere."

What I didn't predict in that article at the turn of the century was the launch of the smartphone, which made the internet portable and constantly accessible for individuals without the need for additional screens on fridge magnets or petrol pumps. The idea of constantly consuming information that is available everywhere, however, for better or worse has become the norm.

The final year of the century also saw me undergo a strange transformation that came as quite a shock.

Chris, Alexander and I had spent one Sunday afternoon outside a restaurant opposite our local cricket green enjoying a leisurely Italian meal and basking in spring sunshine. The following day, I glanced at the living room mirror and noticed a small patch of white skin just above the bridge of my nose. I showed it to Chris, who was just as puzzled as I was by its appearance. We thought little more of it, until other similar patches began to appear over the following few weeks.

I made an appointment with the GP who diagnosed one of two conditions, either tinea versicolor or vitiligo. First, he wanted to rule out tinea versicolor, a common fungal infection that grows under the skin and results in small, discoloured patches, similar to the ones I was experiencing.

"I could give you a prescription for a cream," he told me. "But by far the simplest thing is to cover your body from head to toe in a shampoo designed for severe dandruff."

He sent me off to buy the shampoo, apply it liberally and leave it on for a day, repeating the process 24 hours later.

Deciding the procedure would be best carried out on a weekend, the following Saturday, while standing in the bath, I opened the bottle and began to administer the shampoo, which turned out to be bright orange in colour.

Covered in the lotion, I let it dry. Then having decided I wasn't going to let the situation affect my normal weekend plans, headed out to a nearby pub garden where Chris and I regularly enjoyed a lunchtime drink while five-year-old Alexander explored the play area.

I entered the garden through a small side gate, hat pulled over my face and head bowed, and we made our way to a table as far away from other customers as possible.

As I sat, glowing orange and looking like the character who had been "Tangoed" in the nineties soft-drink TV ads, for an instant I began to wonder whether the whole scenario was a crazy wind-up by the GP. Was he at that very moment recounting to his golfing buddies the story of how he talked a naive patient into covering himself in fluorescent orange shampoo for two days?

The worst moment of the weekend came on the Saturday evening when Manchester United lifted the FA Cup, one of three trophies they won that season, and a tiny tear appeared in the corner of my eye as I took in the momentous events on TV. As the droplet mixed with the shampoo, the trickle of tears turned into a flood and the stinging burning sensation left me in agony.

For all the pain and humiliation, the shampoo had no effect on the patches. When I returned to the GP the following week, he confirmed that I was suffering from vitiligo, a skin condition caused by a lack of melanin, the pigment in skin. It's probably best known as the condition that Michael Jackson claimed had turned his face white.

There's no known cure for vitiligo, which can cause white patches to appear anywhere on the body and can cause embarrassment for some people, especially if the affected area is on the face. Luckily, and unusually, my vitiligo affected my entire body, slowly stripping me of pigment from head to toe but in the end giving my skin a uniform pale white colour.

# CHAPTER 14

The growing digital revolution resulted in a major upheaval in the media industry just a few days into the new millennium. On 10 January 2000, AOL, the US online service with over 30 million subscribers worldwide, announced it was buying Time Warner, the media giant with extensive holdings in cable, movies and publishing, making it the biggest merger in US corporate history.

The deal was completed 12 months later and was to have a major influence on my career, when as part of an aggressive spending spree the new combined company's magazine division, Time Inc, bought IPC Media from its private equity owners, Cinven, for £1.15 billion.

The new US bosses outlined their plans for digital development and made it plain that online strategy would be the responsibility of AOL in the UK. In common with the huge hopes generated by the merger itself, the plans never saw the light of day, and IPC's digital development began to falter.

At the time, it looked like my opportunity to shape a digital future for the company was fading. So when I was asked to move back into the world of print with a newly launched internet-focussed magazine, *Web User*, I jumped at the opportunity to combine my love of print magazines and technology.

*Web User*, the first fortnightly magazine targeting the growing interest in the internet and computers, had launched in the spring of 2001 and seemed perfectly placed to exploit the fact that the internet was becoming mainstream.

Early sales had been disappointing, however. With my dual knowledge of print publishing and the internet, I was asked to transform the magazine from the nerdy publication it had become to a mass market title offering a guide to the fast-growing number of new internet sites, similar to the way *TV Times* highlighted new TV content.

Sales figures began to grow and, with the help of a bright enthusiastic young team, the magazine returned to the course the company had planned for it.

Less than six months after I took over at *Web User*, however, the editor's job at *What's On TV* became vacant. *What's On* was at the time the UK's best-selling magazine, shifting an amazing 1,666,475 copies every week, and by far the IPC's largest profit earner.

With my background in TV magazines, it seemed to be too good an opportunity to resist, so I applied for the job and was successful. It was a huge responsibility, but I relished the challenge.

My insight across both the print and digital editorial operations now put me in a unique position within the company and very soon I was elected as the chairman of IPC's Editors' Group. The group, composed of the company's senior editors, met monthly. As well as helping the board with major editorial decisions, its main role was to organise a yearly editors' conference and annual editorial awards.

The awards were an impressive affair, held at the Grosvenor House Hotel in Park Lane, hosted by a major TV celebrity such as Jonathan Ross or Rob Brydon, and were attended by the editorial teams of all 100 or so magazines.

Judging was done in the month prior to the awards ceremony on the top floor of King's Reach Tower and, as well as editors and publishers from the company, a selection of guest judges helped choose the winners.

A morning spent judging the in-house magazine awards was usually fun. One particular occasion, sharing the task of judging "Scoop of the Year" with celebrity publicist Max Clifford, was also to prove enlightening.

We were sat opposite each other on the 29th floor of the IPC Media building in a small room, with a floor-to-ceiling view of the London skyline at one end. Our first award entry was from the lads' mag *Loaded*. One of their writers had bumped into George Best's ex, Angie, in a London club one evening and gained an exclusive interview about her life with the footballer.

"Well, it's a good-enough story but it would have been better if he'd said she told him George used to wear her knickers," suggested Clifford.

I looked puzzled, as it was obvious from the feature that hadn't happened.

"I would have said, she told me he used to get a thrill from it. That's the bit that would have made the story memorable,' he continued.

"It's like David Mellor and Antonia de Sancha," he said, referring to the tabloid expose about the former Tory cabinet minister's affair with an actress. "What do the public remember about that story? It's him screwing her in a Chelsea shirt. I added that bit," he boasted proudly.

I looked over at his self-satisfied smiling face. It had taken only 10 minutes together but I knew immediately I disliked this man intensely.

"I think we should award him the prize for *not* making up the story," I argued. "He's a journalist, not a novelist."

It was obvious that our philosophies were diametrically opposed. We spent the remainder of the morning uncomfortably sharing the small room, discussing other award entries but very rarely making eye contact.

Little did I guess how loathsome a creature he actually was, as the nation was to discover a number of years later when he was jailed for a series of sexual offences as part of Operation Yewtree, which was set up in the wake of the

234

Jimmy Savile sexual abuse scandal.

I was lucky enough to win an IPC Media award myself on a few occasions – not, I must add, when I was chair of the judges – and despite it being an in-house event it was still a huge thrill.

The editors' conference was also a big annual event, usually held in a grand country house hotel and attended by all the company's editors and senior publishing teams. As well as presentations on subjects such as cover design and editorial innovations from fellow editors, external speakers were invited from areas as diverse as sport, politics and entertainment. One year it might be the chef Heston Blumenthal, another year athlete Sebastian Coe, who at the time had just led the successful bid for the 2012 London Olympics.

One guest who stands out from my time helping to organise the event was Dick Stolley, who told the conference the amazing story of how he secured the only film of the moment President John F Kennedy was assassinated, the infamous Zapruder film. I was lucky enough to be able to chat to him about that day after his speech.

Dick was the founding editor of Time Inc's hugely successful *People* magazine, but at the time of the Kennedy shooting he was Los Angeles bureau chief for *Life*, the company's general-interest magazine known for the quality of its photojournalism.

As he recounted what has been described as the journalistic coup of the twentieth century to the room full of publishing executives, you could hear a pin drop. Dick told how within an hour of hearing the awful news of the attempt on the president's life, he was on a plane to Dallas, only hearing that Kennedy had died once the plane was in the air.

Having arrived in Texas and set up a command centre

at a downtown hotel, Dick received a call from a stringer, or part-time reporter, who was at Dallas police headquarters where the assassin Lee Harvey Oswald was being interviewed. Whispering into the phone, she told Dick that she'd had a tip-off from a local police officer that the assassination had been captured on 8mm film by a local garment manufacturer, whose name she was sure began with a "Z".

Dick reached for the phone book in his hotel room and, running his finger down the Zs, the name "Zapruder, Abraham" jumped out at him. He called the number, but got no reply, so he continued to ring every 15 minutes until, around 11.00 pm, the phone was answered by a tired voice. It was Zapruder himself.

It transpired that Zapruder had been driving around Dallas since the events he'd witnessed at Dealey Plaza, trying to calm himself, and had only just returned home. He'd reported his film of the day's events to Dallas police but, with Oswald already in custody, there appeared to be little interest in it at the time. Zapruder had taken the 8mm film to a Kodak lab in Dallas to be processed, however, and he now had the original and three copies.

In their late-night phone conversation, he confirmed to Dick that the film showed every moment of the fateful shooting. Dick was the first journalist to contact him but he declined Dick's suggestion that he come over to his house at that late hour, instead arranging for him to visit his office at nine o'clock the following morning.

I sat listening to the journalistic legend in complete silence as he continued his incredible story, amazed at how fresh he made it sound, despite the fact he must have recounted it innumerable times.

Dick explained that the following morning he arrived at the garment seller's office an hour early, at eight, being aware other reporters would almost certainly have learnt about the existence of the film. A rather annoyed Zapruder let him in, nonetheless, and Dick found himself in the hallway with two Secret Service agents, who had arrived to view the awful events that had led to the death of their president.

Zapruder showed them into his office, darkened the room and switched on his noisy 8mm projector. Dick described the fearful anticipation he and the two Secret Service men experienced, holding their breath as the film began to run. A shiver ran down my spine as I imagined the silent film screening on the office wall, with only the clicking sound of the celluloid feeding through the gate breaking the hush.

He recounted seeing for the first time the opening scene of onlookers awaiting the visitors from Washington, the motorcade coming into view, the moment the first bullet hits President Kennedy, the second shot hitting Governor Connally, and then the shocking moment he witnessed the sickening sight of the top of Kennedy's head being blown off in frame 313, a photo that was initially withheld from publication.

Dick told us that he knew at that moment *Life* magazine had to have the film. It was, he concluded at the time, unlikely that another complete record of the assassination existed, and he was right.

As the film ended, Dick could hear a gaggle of reporters on the other side of the door. Zapruder showed the film a second time to the new arrivals but agreed to talk to him first. It was Dick's one and only chance to buy possibly the most unique piece of history ever filmed.

Zapruder's biggest worry was that the record of the president's death would be exploited by the media organisation that bought it, but Dick reassured him that *Life* magazine and Time Inc would treat the film with respect. From that point, the deal took very little time, and Dick snuck out the back door of the factory with the original film and a copy, having agreed a fee of $50,000 for the print rights. The following day, he returned and agreed a further $150,000 for the print and motion picture rights.

As the ageing editor came to the end of his story, the room rose as one to salute one of the great journalists of the twentieth century and to applaud his amazing story.

Dick and I chatted later about some of the conspiracy theories surrounding the assassination, many of which include the role of the Zapruder film, with some even incriminating Dick himself in the plot. It was fascinating. I can safely say that listening to Dick and my discussions with astronaut Jim Irwin are the two most fascinating conversations of my entire career.

Another highlight of the editors' conferences were the late-night drinking sessions in the hotel bar. Working in a high-rise building with 29 storeys meant that IPC editors had little opportunity to socialise, except in the lifts taking them to and from their daily schedules. The annual conference gave us the chance to get to know each other under more relaxed circumstances.

I have warm memories of discussing football with Colin Mitchell, editor of my favourite boyhood comic *Shoot*, and watching James Brown, who launched lads' mag *Loaded*, attempting to play snooker after one drink too many and doing severe damage to the table's green baize. I even spent one late-night session with *Railway* magazine editor Nick Piggott passionately discussing train line gauges, a subject that before that drunken night I had no interest in whatsoever, and a topic unsurprisingly I've never discussed since.

One of the most fascinating conversations I enjoyed while burning the midnight oil was with Allan Jones, the editor of the music and film monthly *Uncut*. Coincidentally it concerned another infamous twentieth century shooting.

Welsh-born Allan was quiet-spoken but had long shoulder-length hair that made him stand out in any room. He had joined music weekly *Melody Maker* in the mid-seventies, and by the time I first met him in the early nineties he was already a legend in music writing circles.

I and another three or four editors were enjoying a libation in the smart bar of our hotel with him after a full day of conference sessions, when one of the group mentioned he'd heard a story that Allan was in part responsible for the death of John Lennon. The mention of the infamous killing outside New York's Dakota Building immediately captured everyone's attention and we pressed Allan for details of his involvement.

What followed was a story I'd never heard before, involving a short-lived feud between Lennon and fellow sixties rock star Todd Rundgren, sparked by an interview Allan had conducted in 1974.

During the interview, Rundgren had lashed out at the Liverpudlian star, calling him a hypocrite, claiming he had a history of dubious behaviour, particularly towards women, and criticising the lack of creativity displayed by the Beatles compared to his own band Nazz.

Lennon had hit back, publishing an open letter to Rundgren, who he referred to in the missive as "Turd Runtgreen". It was this letter and its contents that many allege started Lennon's killer Mark Chapman, a massive Todd Rundgren fan who even wore a Rundgren T-shirt as he fired the fatal shot, on his murderous road.

That night, Allan admitted to the group of us in the bar that the original article had been angled to create a headline-grabbing story. In that respect, it had undoubtedly succeeded. But the question was: Had it produced unintended consequences that six years later had rocked the world?

Everything was going well at work and at home, with Alexander about to enter his final months of primary school. Then in December 2004, we received a terrifying message from Ian, who was appearing in pantomime at the Pavilion Theatre in Glasgow.

The Pavilion was the theatre where he and Janette had first met, when he was a lighting engineer and she was a teenager in panto. Since 1998, The Krankies had topped the bill in the theatre's Christmas show many times, and in 2004 the production was *Jack and the Beanstalk*.

I picked up the phone to hear an emotional Ian explaining there had been a terrible accident. That afternoon, as the first half of the show ended and the curtains began to close, Janette had been waving to the audience from the top of a stage lift, which was dressed to look like the beanstalk, when the lift collapsed.

"I heard a crack and then the whole beanstalk just gave way and Janette fell 20 feet onto the stage," he told me, holding back his tears.

Janette had been taken to Glasgow Royal Infirmary, and Ian sat at her bedside until she regained consciousness. She later confessed her last memories were of Ian, dressed as a pantomime dame with a huge wig and rouged cheeks, screaming, "Don't touch her, don't move her," before she blanked out completely.

Ian admitted that as he saw blood trickling from his partner's ear he thought she was dead. The blood, it turned out, was from a burst eardrum, and she also suffered broken ribs, a broken collar bone and damage to her chest wall. The biggest threat to her life, though, was a fracture to her skull.

Those first few hours and days were horrific, as we waited to discover first of all if Janette would survive, and later whether the cracked skull would have any long-term effects. Thankfully, there were no ongoing problems resulting from the fall, but it was some time before Janette

240

revived her role as the schoolboy Jimmy, missing pantomime the following year but returning triumphantly in 2006 at the age of 60.

My funniest memory of what was a horrific time for Ian and the family was the mention Jonathan Ross made of the events in the monologue that opened his BBC1 chat show the following Friday night.

"Did you see Janette Krankie had a terrifying fall from a beanstalk in pantomime this week?" he asked the audience. "The ambulance staff were very confused; they didn't know whether to take her to the geriatric ward or the children's ward!"

Bizarrely, exactly 10 years later, my other sister-in-law, Jean, also found herself in the Glasgow Royal Infirmary after a major accident involving a fall, one that was to lead to her death... and subsequent resurrection.

Jean had been a dancer with the Moxen Girls, a dance troupe that provided showgirls for theatres across Scotland and beyond in the days of variety theatre. My brother Alistair had met her at the Pavilion Theatre when Ian worked on the lighting board, and the pair had married and moved to Rothesay on the Isle of Bute, down the Clyde from Glasgow.

Alistair owned an estate agent / insurance agent / travel agent business, while Jean ran the local wool shop, and they brought up my lovely nieces, Ailsa and Shona, on the beautiful island.

At one point, Jean also ran a dancing school. One of her pupils was Lena Zavaroni, the daughter of a local Rothesay chip shop owner, who became a national singing sensation in the seventies when she won the talent show *Opportunity Knocks*.

On the day of her accident, Alistair and Jean were walking through Glasgow Central Station, after returning from visiting their daughter Ailsa in London, when Jean fell forwards and banged her head on the concourse of the station. A passing doctor came to her rescue and, finding no pulse, began to give her CPR. He managed to restart her heart but she still hadn't regained consciousness by the time she reached the hospital.

Days went by and Jean showed no signs of awakening. Chris, Alexander and I were due to fly to Florida for a two-week holiday. After an emotional telephone conversation with Alistair, in which he encouraged us to continue with our plans, as there was nothing we could do to help Jean, we headed to the States. We awoke every morning hoping for a text message with good news but none arrived.

Eventually, the doctors ran a rigorous series of tests to check for electrical brain activity and, finding absolutely none, sadly recommended the life support systems be switched off.

Alistair made the heart-breaking decision to donate Jean's organs for transplant – a decision that was to save her life.

In preparation for her organs being harvested, as the process was called, the nurse began to remove Jean's nail varnish. As she did so, she observed one of Jean's eyes blink. It was the start of an amazing recovery that saw Jean out of bed and walking within a day and eventually released from hospital.

The doctors described Jean as "a walking miracle" and had no explanation as to how a brain-dead woman could return to almost full strength. While she didn't see the white tunnel of light that some patients often describe when they suffer a near-death experience, Jean revealed later that she did have a strange vision while unconscious, involving Lorenzo Amoruso, the former captain of Rangers, the football club she and Alistair supported.

"I kept thinking I'd seen Amoruso stepping out of a taxi,"

she later admitted, "and I'd slipped in the street because he's such a good-looking man. But it was all in my imagination."

Tragically, the story doesn't have a completely happy ending. As Jean was undergoing a final set of tests, just before she was discharged, the hospital discovered that the cancer she had bravely fought a number of years earlier had returned.

The miraculous recovery she had undergone gave her a number of extra years to spend with Alistair, Shona, Ailsa and her granddaughters, Isla and Holly, but a few years later she sadly died from the effects of the cancer.

Twelve years after I launched *TV & Satellite Week*, TV magazine sales continued to flourish, and our German competitor, Bauer, had successfully launched two new titles into the market, *TV Choice* and *Total TV Guide*. So in 2005, in an attempt to defend its share of the market, IPC asked me to develop a new weekly TV magazine.

We created a variety of propositions and put them into research, from a glossy upmarket guide to a more downmarket tabloid-focussed title, from a larger page size to a small format magazine.

In the end, we received a strong message from the research sessions – that a compact guide was preferred – and in late spring, *TV easy*, a magazine about half the size of *What's On TV*, hit the shelves. I oversaw the launch as editor-in-chief, while Richard Clark, who I'd worked with for a number of years and who had replaced me at *Web User*, became the day-to-day editor.

The magazine's launch coincided with the annual *British Soap Awards* ceremony on ITV, so we decided to sponsor the after-show party as a way of introducing the title to the stars of the soaps, shows that formed a major element of *TV easy*. I'd been invited to be a judge for the awards a couple of years before and continued to be part of the judging panel for many years, becoming at one time the longest-serving jury member.

The work started in early spring, when a huge box of video tapes (later DVDs) would arrive by courier. Each video would feature one of the categories – from *Best Comedy Performance* to *Best On-screen Partnership*, *Spectacular Scene of the Year* to *Best Storyline*. In total, the jury would judge 10 or 11 categories, while the viewers would vote for the remainder of the 16 awards, through forms in *The Sun* newspaper and *What's On TV*.

The soaps submitted video entries for their nominees, each about three minutes long. So with six or seven soaps entered for each category, the amount of time that needed to be spent assessing the performances and writing comments about each one added up to almost a day's work.

Once that stage was completed, the judges met to debate the winners. Initially these meetings took place in London, at ITV's London Studios on the South Bank, but later the judging day took into account the regional aspect of the soaps and was shared by cities such as Manchester and Birmingham.

The judging days could be quite supercharged events, as the executive producers of the soaps were included in the discussions and understandably felt passionate about their show's claims. In addition, there was also an equal number of "TV experts" on the panel, of which I was one.

In those early days on London's South Bank, the judging panel would convene in a large airy conference room about halfway up the 24-floor London Studios building, with a wonderful view over the river Thames. The awards show executive producer would act as chairman, and before each vote a short video would be played, featuring clips of the six or seven nominees. Next, one or two of the judges were asked to give their opinions on the performances, before finally the discussion was opened up to the room.

The votes were intriguing, involving stealthy horse trading, tactical voting and a great deal of emotion. I remember the executive producer of one of the country's biggest soaps accusing another of "taking the easy option by playing the cancer card" with one of his characters, before realising that his outburst in front of the astonished jury had probably lost his nominee the award.

After the discussion, each member of the judging panel was given a voting slip by a representative of a third-party legal firm, who would collect the completed papers and retire to a separate room to count the votes. The jury then had to wait until the awards ceremony itself to find out who had triumphed.

As a judge, I was always invited to the awards night itself and the infamous party after the show, where celebrities let their hair down, along with their inhibitions. Trouserless young stars dancing on the piano, sozzled soap divas arguing with rivals before collapsing in a heap, and the party almost brought to a halt by a barrage of stink bombs dropped by Keith Lemon star Leigh Francis, are among the many unforgettable moments.

Another star-studded annual event I enjoyed attending was the *TV Times Carols with the Stars* celebration at the Royal Albert Hall. I'd first attended it during my initial spell at *TV Times* but when I took over as editor of *What's On TV*, I had the added fun of hosting a box at the beautiful Victorian concert hall.

The celebrity carol concert was held every year in early December in aid of Bloodwise, the blood cancer charity, and brought together television stars from all aspects of TV. It was first held in the late 1970s, when the charity was known as Leukaemia Research. Over the years, it had become a harbinger of Christmas, for not only the teams at the TV magazines but also for a huge range of stars who looked forward to the event every year.

As the host of a box, I was expected to ensure my celebrity guests always had a full glass of champagne as they sat enjoying the show from the plush burgundy velvet seats above the auditorium. It wasn't a tough job, in any way.

Over the years, I was lucky to entertain a selection of mainly friendly down-to-earth personalities, which for some unaccountable reason seemed to include a higher-than-average proportion of actors who played TV cops.

Graham Cole, the reliable PC Tony Stamp in *The Bill*, was the first, followed by a squad of others, including John Michie, *Taggart*'s DI Robbie Ross and later *Holby* CEO Guy Self, Stephen Tompkinson, DCI Banks in the series of the same name, Kevin Whateley, *Morse*'s sidekick Inspector Lewis, and Caroline Quentin, DCI Janine Lewis in *Blue Murder*.

Typical of many of the actors and celebrities I hosted at the Albert Hall, Caroline was extremely nervous before going on stage. As I sat next to her, my first impression was that she was somewhat aloof, conversing in short sentences and not interacting with other guests in the box. Just before the interval, she headed down the corridor from the box to wait in the wings for her cue.

Returning to the box after introducing a carol, she immediately apologised for her earlier demeanour. "I was just so nervous going up on that iconic stage, I couldn't relax," she revealed.

Soap stars were also regular visitors to the box, with Barbara Windsor and Jo Joyner from *EastEnders* enjoying the occasion, and two other Albert Square actors, Cheryl Ferguson and Linda Henry, the soap's Shirley and Heather, even harmonising to sing *Happy Birthday* to my teenage son Alexander one year.

*Emmerdale*'s Lorraine Chase was another soap favourite we hosted one Christmas. She had worked in pantomime in Bournemouth with Ian and Janette the previous year and, having introduced ourselves and with endless bubbly flowing, she, Chris and I quickly began to enjoy a party atmosphere. So, when another guest, former newsreader Angela Rippon, the first female journalist to present the news on the BBC, arrived at the door of the box, I threw my arms around her, in typical showbiz luvvy fashion, and greeted her with a kiss on both cheeks.

She recoiled in alarm at my over-effusive welcome, and I suddenly realised that I had been a little too over-familiar with a woman I'd never met before. What could have been an awkward moment with a national treasure was saved, however, by Chris who, seeing the sticky situation I'd got myself into, followed up with a similar dual-cheek embrace. Her kindred greeting appeared to assure Angela that we were simply a very affectionate couple!

Others whose company I enjoyed over the many years I attended the annual event included entrepreneur and fellow Clydebank boy Duncan Bannatyne, style guru Laurence Llewellyn Bowen, chef Gary Rhodes and impressionist Jon Culshaw, who spent the bulk of the night conversing in other people's voices.

One of my favourite Albert Hall guests was former BBC political correspondent John Sergeant, who had recently launched an entertainment career making a name for himself in *Strictly Come Dancing*.

John recalled the night he was outside the British Embassy in Paris in 1990 when news that Margaret Thatcher had lost the first round of the Conservative Party leadership election came through. Broadcasting live from the steps of the embassy, John was interrupted by the then prime minister, who appeared behind him leaving the building.

He attempted to ask her, "Mrs Thatcher, could I ask you for a comment?"

At that point, Thatcher's aides, including her burly press

secretary Sir Bernard Ingham, bundled poor John aside as she began an impromptu press conference, side-lining the BBC reporter, who looked bemused and confused on the edge of the scrum of journalists that immediately formed.

I'd heard John recount his highly amusing version of the story on Radio 4 just the week before, but I couldn't resist asking him to retell it for me and the other guests in the box, in the same way you might request a great poet recite a favourite verse.

My own personal encounters with British politicians have thrown up a number of interesting surprises.

I was first invited to 10 Downing Street, as a member of the British Society of Magazine Editors, in the noughties, when Tony Blair was prime minister. Keen to boost his election chances, he realised magazine articles offered him a softer access point to the British public than the mostly hostile, national newspapers. He set up a meeting with the country's editors in order to mount a charm offensive.

It was disconcerting entering a door I'd seen so many times on television, and climbing the main staircase lined with engravings and photos of each of our prime ministers, from Walpole to John Major.

Blair entered the spacious Pillard Room, dominated by a huge portrait of Elizabeth I, and began to work the space like the consummate politician he is. He appeared rather ill at ease, however, aware that no end of briefings could have prepared him for the range of questions a room full of experts like the one he was facing could dish up for him.

Like most of the editors who attended, I had a brief chat with him and enjoyed the opportunity to explore hidden parts of Downing Street normally off-limits to the general public.

Much less guarded was Gordon Brown, Blair's immediate successor. I first met him at a reception in the

Chancellor of the Exchequer's residence, 11 Downing Street, a few months before he moved next door to take over as prime minister. I was amazed how unlike the dour Scot caricature painted by the media he was.

We chatted for some time about Scottish football, in particular his own team Raith Rovers, and cricket, another passion of his. I told him I was planning to head straight home after the reception to watch Scotland play in a Cricket World Cup match. He suggested that, given our home nation's record in international sporting tournaments, I'd better leave immediately as the game wouldn't last long.

Throughout the event, he was charming and funny and the antithesis of the cold-hearted morose character he was most often portrayed as. I frequently ponder if the Labour PR machine had done a better job of illustrating his human side, could we have dodged the David Cameron era and the horrors of Brexit it bequeathed us.

My first encounter with Cameron himself was in his days as leader of the opposition, although I was later invited to a reception with him in Downing Street after his victory in the 2010 General Election. Taking some pages out of Blair and Brown's playbook by cosying up to the magazine industry, Cameron invited a group of BSME editors to a drinks party in his rooms in Portcullis House, the building that provides extra office space for parliamentarians.

A former PR man for Carlton TV, which held the ITV London daytime franchise for a number of years, he was a very smooth character, who always seemed to have the right answer for his audience.

I arrived a little early at Portcullis House, sharing a taxi from our offices just across the Thames with Conor McNicholas, the editor of the music paper *New Musical Express* (or *NME*, as it had been rebranded).

Having undergone a stringent security check on the ground floor, we took the lift up to Cameron's office, a bright modern room, and found we were the first of the party to arrive. Accepting a glass of wine from one of the staff, we began to look around the room, when Cameron walked in behind us.

We introduced ourselves, and when Conor revealed he was the editor of the *NME*, Cameron's face lit up.

"We used to share one copy around our school dorm," he enthused. "There was a huge fight every week to be the first to read it." It was obvious Cameron had an affection for Conor's publication.

Introducing myself as the editor of *What's On TV*, I reckoned the Tory leader wouldn't have the same affinity with my magazine's subject matter. "I don't suppose you get much time to watch TV," I suggested to him.

"No, I often curl up on the settee with my official papers and watch a good detective drama at the weekend," he answered quickly.

I could see from Conor's gaze that he, like me, was sceptical about the response and thought this was Cameron's attempt to come across as a man of the people, so he pushed him further on his answer.

"Did you see *A Touch of Frost* last night," Conor asked, slyly, referring to the David Jason murder mystery that had aired the previous evening.

"Yes, very good," said Cameron.

"Who did you think did it?" countered Conor.

That's it, I thought, he's got you.

Surprisingly, however, Cameron then went into a long explanation of who he had suspected was the murderer and why. We were both taken aback and a little ashamed that we'd doubted his sincerity.

It turns out that Cameron's love of detective series actually played a major role in British diplomacy during his years as PM. Having got off to a rocky start, his relationship

250

with German chancellor Angela Merkel was, some claim, forged over a shared enthusiasm for *Midsomer Murders*!

As a young local newspaper editor in the early eighties, I used to get a huge kick out of hailing a taxi in the courtyard of the House of Commons after dining with the local Clydebank MP and savouring the late-night journey through the quite-dark streets of Westminster from the Houses of Parliament, past Downing Street, up the Mall and around the Queen Victoria Monument, with its excellent view of Buckingham Palace. As I've said, it was the perfect heritage tour of London.

I never guessed on those late-night journeys that one day later in my career I might visit not just the great Downing Street houses, but also the Queen's London residence. The invitation to Buckingham Palace was for the launch of a David Attenborough documentary about climate change and deforestation, *The Queen's Green Planet*.

Chris and I had visited St James's Palace many years before for a Childline reception, hosted by the Duchess of Wessex, at which the actor John Hurt had read a poem about a young child suffering abuse that was so moving almost the entire room was in tears. But from both a scale and grandeur aspect, the royal home at the end of the Mall was on another level.

As we left Buckingham Palace, each of the attendees was given a small hazel tree in a plastic bag – a personal gift from the Queen, we were informed. Leaving the Grand Entrance, crossing the inner Quadrangle and heading towards the archway that faced the main gates bustling on the other side with tourists, I proudly planned a spot in the front garden where I would plant the tiny tree, envisaging one day telling generations to come that the huge 15-foot tree it would grow into had begun its days at Buckingham Palace.

Unfortunately, without the care of a royal gardener, the hazel tree failed to flourish and by the end of the summer all that could be seen was a dead dry stick that looked decidedly unregal. Sorry Your Majesty!

I've been lucky enough to visit some amazing places that most people could only dream of, from Buckingham Palace and Downing Street to the sets of leading TV shows, and I've met a vast range of fascinating characters along the way. So, people regularly ask me, "Who's the most interesting person you've met?"

Looking back through a list of showbiz personalities, footballers, politicians, a man who walked on the moon and our future king, one man stands out for overcoming a disability that would have devastated most other human beings, and for the legacy left by his brilliant mind. Unfortunately, my encounter with the genius Stephen Hawking involved me proving to be far from intelligent.

I'd been invited to the launch of *Into the Universe*, a TV series written by Hawking, at the Royal Society. I took along Alexander, who at the time was a teenager. We entered the impressive building in London's St James, where we met up with a number of members of the *What's On TV* team and watched the first episode of the series, followed by a fascinating talk by Hawking about space, time travel and the possibility of alien life.

Afterwards, while enjoying a drink in the opulent early nineteenth-century building, Jo Lewis, the magazine's features editor, noticed the professor was alone. "Has anyone got a camera," she asked. "We could get a photo with him."

In those days, before smartphones were ubiquitous, I carried a small disposable camera in my bag in case a photo opportunity arose. "I've got one," I offered, at which point Jo purposefully strode over to ask one of Professor

Hawking's support team if a photo would be possible.

After he consulted with Professor Hawking, we were given the all-clear. The team and Alexander began to gather round the great man's wheelchair, as I readied myself to snap the image. Embarrassingly, whether it was nerves or a genuine problem with the small camera, I couldn't get the thing to work. I stood there fiddling with the device, sold as being the simplest of cameras, to no avail.

I searched through my bag for a second camera but found nothing. I returned to the original one and tried to wind on the film… nothing happened.

All through my trials, the team stood beaming expectantly behind Professor Hawking as he, head to one side, stared directly at me.

After what seemed like an eternity, the professor's assistant stepped in, motioned for me to join the group behind the chair, took the camera from me and painlessly took a snapshot, wound on the camera, took a second and handed it back to me. No hassle, job done.

We thanked the professor profusely for the photo and headed off. As he watched us walk away, I could only imagine what the world-leading theoretical physicist made of the gibbering idiot he'd just encountered, who couldn't even work a point-and-click camera.

# CHAPTER 15

I celebrated 40 years as a journalist in 2017, and I could truthfully say that I'd enjoyed every one of the various roles I'd embraced.

The number of magazines sold under my editorship was well north of one billion copies and I'd won numerous in-house awards and the Milia d'Or at the Cannes New Media Festival, and *What's On TV* had received a prestigious Periodical Publishers Association prize for its ongoing success.

One thing ever so slightly bugged me, however – I'd never won a British Society of Magazine Editors award. Since my first nomination in the early nineties, when as editor of *TV Guide* I'd looked around the table at my expectant colleagues and celebrated my premature success only to lose out in the most embarrassing of ways, I'd been nominated 14 times without a win.

I knew the TV magazines I'd edited were too mass-market for the tastes of the majority of those who sat on judging panels, but they were successful – often selling more in one week than many winners of the awards would sell in their lifetime.

So as the years went by, I convinced myself that awards didn't matter and I'd proved my worth by the sheer bulk of magazines I'd sold. Deep down, however, I knew it niggled away at me.

As the call for entries for the awards came around again in the summer of 2018, I was in two minds whether to submit an entry or not. Assuming another shortlisting without a win would at least gain me some kind of record, I allowed my name to be put forward once more.

I was shortlisted again. On the night of the awards at the

Sheraton Grand in Park Lane, I sat next to my friend and colleague Mark Hedges, the editor of *Country Life*, another regular shortlist candidate who deservedly regularly picked up awards.

The number of attendees had dwindled remarkably since my first awards ceremony in 1993 and the magazine industry was now in steep decline due to the growth of the internet. My colleagues around the table assured me that this would be the year, as was the case each time I was nominated, but I had no more expectation of winning than I had on any of the past dozen occasions.

Amazingly, however, 2018 proved to be my lucky year and I mounted the stage to accept the award from comedian Rachel Parris.

As I left the hotel ballroom that night in late 2018, I felt I had completed a journey.

During the following two years, IPC Media, which had changed its name to TI Media following its purchase by Time Warner, was again sold, this time to Future Publishing, a British-based publishing company that had found a way to make a success of media brands in the internet age.

I was asked to change my role one last time, from editor-in-chief of *TV Times*, *What's On TV* and *TV & Satellite Week* to managing director of the company's TV and film titles. It was a position I was reluctant to commit to, but having agreed with Chris that if I didn't enjoy the job I would take it as a signal to retire, I went ahead with it.

Nine months later, feeling I couldn't spend the final years of my career struggling through endless strategy meetings and spreadsheets, I decided that being managing director was exactly the type of job I'd become a journalist to avoid. I handed in my notice to retire.

It was almost two years to the day after Ian and Janette announced that The Krankies would no longer be appearing in pantomime. Janette had been diagnosed with osteoporosis in 2017 and they both felt that at 72 it was time to hang up the school jacket and cap and retire.

I left full-time employment in March 2021 and spent the summer and autumn doing many of the things that work had precluded me from enjoying. Chris and I attended Wimbledon and several race meetings, my mate Kevin and I attended a couple of Surrey cricket matches, and I visited the theatre and cinema regularly.

I was just considering which events I could plan for the dark winter months, when the discovery of a tumour in my oesophagus rudely interrupted my life of leisure, and its treatment filled my diary for much of 2022.

So it was that at 9 am on Hogmanay 2021, I found myself sitting in a chemotherapy ward at the Royal Surrey County Hospital beginning my first course of treatment for oesophageal cancer.

It was diagnosed at the beginning of December, and the month up until Christmas was taken up with tests and consultations. The plan was for four courses of chemo every two weeks, a break for six to eight weeks, followed by surgery to remove part of my oesophagus and replace it with a portion of my stomach, and then another eight weeks of chemo. The good news was that the scans indicated that the cancer hadn't spread to any major organs.

It had been a rapid journey from diagnosis to the start of treatment, although I first suffered trouble digesting food in July and consulted the GP a few weeks later. That was followed by a series of phone consultations, as face-to-face meetings were suspended at the GP surgery due to the COVID pandemic.

Once the cancer was diagnosed, a new lexicon of acronyms entered my day-to-day life, with PICC lines and FLOT treatments dominating the conversation.

It was the third time that cancer had interrupted our

lives, as my malignant melanoma in the early nineties was followed some years later by Chris being diagnosed with breast cancer. Her regular mammogram showed a small change in the cells, and she had an operation to remove them. Luckily, however, the problem hadn't spread and she was given the all clear.

An ad campaign repeated regularly on TV around the time of my second diagnosis claimed one in two people in the UK will develop cancer. Chris and I both felt we'd done our bit for the statistics.

As the date of my operation grew nearer, it was strange to find myself facing the same dilemma that had confronted my father as he contemplated his heart surgery back in my teenage years. There was a small, yet scary, chance that, like him, I wouldn't survive my time in the operating theatre. In fact, as I recovered in the intensive care unit one of the nurses admitted that the operation had been more complex than open-heart surgery.

Should I leave a letter similar to the one my father prepared for me and my mother, Alistair and Ian, in case the worst happened?

I thought about it long and hard, and even contemplated filming a video to leave with friends to be given to Alexander and Chris in the event of my death.

In the end, I decided against leaving a message from beyond the grave as Dad had done in 1975.

I've always tried to follow his philosophy that the glass is half full not half empty. While I understood how, despite that strongly held belief, he felt he was being a realist rather than a pessimist by writing his final letter to us, I didn't follow his example.

I'm pretty sure that both Chris and Alexander know how dearly I love them. As for offering advice for the future, as Dad did in his letter all those years ago, I know neither of them need any guidance I can offer.

Chris is the most level-headed, sensible person I know, and her kind heart is something I'm so glad to say Alexander has inherited from her. He is growing to be a better man than I am, and I couldn't be more proud to call him my son.

My operation took place the week of Good Friday. I'd had a number of meetings with my consultant and other hospital members of staff, who gave me details of what could go wrong, including the chance of not surviving. Thankfully the surgery went smoothly and I was out of hospital less than 10 days after the operation.

The week after my surgery, I met with the consultant to hear how the operation had gone and to discover the results of the biopsy of the oesophagus and the 59 surrounding nodes that had been removed. The amazing news was that the first round of chemo had totally eradicated the cancer and there was no sign of it anywhere.

It was better news than I could have hoped for but, despite that, seven weeks after my release from hospital, the chemotherapy started again. A belt-and-braces exercise, I'd been assured, to ensure that all traces of the cancer had been destroyed.

The first course of chemo had been relatively gentle on my body; the support drugs provided by the oncology team had lessened, or even eliminated in some cases, many of the worst side effects of the treatment. The second course of four cycles, two weeks apart, hit me much harder, including three days of constant, agonising stomach cramps after the first cycle. Tweaks were made to the chemo drugs, however, and things settled down somewhat.

The effects of the chemo were not helped by the vagaries of the British weather, which served up a summer of extraordinary record-breaking temperatures, leading to me twice enduring 40°C heat on the third and fourth days after treatment when I was at my most delicate.

Having said my body coped well with the chemo

sessions, when I look back I can list 20 side effects that I suffered from the treatment – cramps; discoloured and warped nails; bad sleep; loss of hair; loss of taste; loss of appetite; diarrhoea; tingling in the feet; muscle twitches in the legs; a swollen tongue; nausea; a sore throat; severe sensitivity to cold drinks; sensitivity to cold on the skin; a runny nose; weeping eyes; abdominal pains; a red rash on face; exhaustion; hiccups (lasting up to eight hours).

While it sounds like a horrendous burden, surprisingly it was all copeable, the worst of the lot being loss of taste, which made eating and drinking, both vital following the operation to prevent weight loss, a particularly difficult process. Even water tasted bitter and metallic.

By August, however, four months after the operation, I was beginning to resume a normal life, enjoying a picnic on the Thames with friends and celebrating my recovery by hiring a box at Kempton races.

I had dodged the bullet and I decided to simply add the months of illness and treatment to the many interesting experiences I'd encountered in a packed life and career.

# Acknowledgments

Thanks to:
David Richardson for his design genius.
Victoria Goldman for her proofreading skills.
Cathy Rentzenbrink for passing on her memoir writing wisdom.
Matt Bendoris and Neil Bailey for their publishing advice
Friends and family for their encouragement.